DARK KNIGHTS AND
DINGY CASTLES

HORRIBLE HISTORIES

DARK KNIGHTS AND DINGY CASTLES

Terry Deary Illustrated by Philip Reeve

SCHOLASTIC

For Laura Ritzema

Scholastic Children's Books,
Euston House, 24 Eversholt Street,
London NW1 1DB, UK

A division of Scholastic Ltd
London ~ New York ~ Toronto ~ Sydney ~ Auckland
Mexico City ~ New Delhi ~ Hong Kong

First published in the UK by Scholastic Ltd, 1997
This edition published by Scholastic Ltd, 2017

Text © Terry Deary, 1997
Illustrations © Philip Reeve, 1997
Cover illustration © Martin Brown, 2011

ISBN 978 1407 17982 7

Page layout services provided by Quadrum Solutions Ltd, Mumbai, India
Printed and bound in the UK by CPI Group (UK) Ltd, Croydon, CR0 4YY

4 6 8 10 9 7 5 3

The right of Terry Deary, Philip Reeve and Martin Brown to be identified as the author and illustrators of this work respectively has been
asserted by them in accordance with the Copyright, Designs and Patents Act, 1988.

Papers used by Scholastic Children's Books are made from wood grown in sustainable forests.

www.scholastic.co.uk

CONTENTS

Introduction 7

Timeline 10

Dark knights 15

Terrific tournaments 48

Cruel Crusades 71

Battles and blood 94

Dingy castles 116

Dreadful dungeons 130

Clever castles 138

Creepy castles 145

Savage sieges 156

Epilogue 173

Introduction

History can be horrible. For a start, teachers and parents expect you to learn so much...

The trouble is they try to make it too simple...

And nothing is ever that simple. Take the men of war. If you were rich you rode on a horse, were well fed and fit and would be treated like a gentleman if you fell in battle. If you were poor you'd tramp through freezing mud or choking dust on sore feet, be half-starved and sickly, and if you fell in battle you'd be slaughtered like a turkey at Christmas. Whap!

This book is mainly about the rich blokes on the horses. No, not the boring facts about their *greaves* and *poleyns* but the interesting facts that you really want to know, about the *glaives* and the *pullings*. Because *greaves* and *poleyns* are just metal plates to protect the shins and the knees. You can see rusty, dusty things like that in some old museum. But *glaives* are sharp curved knives on long poles that had hooks on for *pulling* a knight off his horse. The common foot soldiers would use them. Once an armour-plated knight was down on the ground, the foot soldier would use the sharp, pointy end to find a little chink between two plates of armour. He'd work it into the gap till he found a nice soft bit of human being.

If you were a freezing, starving peasant and you had your *glaive* at the neck of a rich, fat man in a can, what would you do? That's what history should be about. People. How did they behave? *Why* did they behave like that? And what would *you* do if you'd been in their shoes … or their *solerets*?

This is the story of soldiers who fought on horseback from around AD 1000 to about 1600 – dangerous men, dark knights. Men who *said* they'd be true to their leader (some hope), polite to everyone (fat chance) and defend the weak (you must be joking).

After about 1600 'knights' were any men or women that the monarch chose to honour. They didn't have to serve the monarch with a sword and a horse – in fact a lot of them couldn't sit on a horse without falling off or hold a sword without dropping it on somebody's foot. So after 1600 knights get about as exciting as two snakes having a boxing match.

This is also the story of the homes they lived in, fought in and fought to *get* in ... their castles. A bungalow at Brighton wasn't good enough for a knight, oh, no. He had to build a posh stone pile with creepy corridors, twisting turrets; bleak buildings from their bloodstained battlements to their dismal, dank and dingy dungeons. Why didn't they settle for a cottage in Cambridge or a flat in Fleetwood? Because they thought a castle was *safe*! But were there ways of cracking open castles and deading desperate defenders? Read on and find out...

Timeline

About AD 500 China. The stirrup is invented. Now warriors can fight on horseback without falling off the saddle.

About AD 1000 France. Norman horsemen stop throwing their spears and start using them underarm to stab. The lance is born. The clever Normans invent chain mail at around the same time.

1041 Winchester. First mention of 'jousting' in England – knights charging at one another with lances for sport.

1050s Europe. Soldiers begin to swear not to hurt women, children or priests ... and not to fight on holy days or between Thursday and Sunday. (That left 80 days a year.) The idea of 'knighthood' starts to grow.

1066 William the Conqueror invades England and his Norman conquerors start building castles with square wooden walls and towers to defend themselves.

1086 England. The Domesday Book describes all the land and lords in England ... but no 'knights' are mentioned. But the king 'dubbed' his son in this year – he touched his shoulders with a sword and the boy became a 'knight'.

1095 Pope Urban II asks for knights to defend the Christian church in Jerusalem and throw out the Turkish rulers. It's the start of the First Crusade.

1096 The Peasants' Crusade, led by Peter the Hermit, sets off for Jerusalem *before* the knights … and most are massacred.

Early 1100s Castles are being made from stone now. 'Tournaments' (that's men battering opponents for fun) turn war into a sport. (Please note: *being* battered is not so much fun.)

1120 The Knights Templars are formed – fighting monks who will protect the pilgrims in Jerusalem.

1130 Pope Innocent II bans tournaments because he thinks the knights should not die fighting … unless it's on his Crusade of course, then it's all right!

1135 Civil War in England. Every powerful man builds his own castle and King Stephen is powerless to stop them.

1145 A Second Crusade is organized and fails pretty miserably. God was supposed to protect Crusaders, so he gets the blame.

1186 Germany. A new law says only the sons of knights can become knights. Euro-peasants stay peasants. But brave English peasants can be knighted by the king.

11

1187 A Third Crusade has lots of great kings (like Richard the Lionheart of England) but does little better than the Second Crusade.

Late 1100s Poems about knights become popular in France Tournaments become respectable.

Early 1200s Knights start fighting in armour plates. Before they'd used chain mail – hard to keep the rust off. The longbow is invented in Wales: one arrow can go through a knight *and* his horse!

1261 The Christians lose Jerusalem, so the Crusades were pointless.

1267 In England Edward I passes laws to control tournaments because the events always cause terrible riots.

1280s Edward I of England starts building 'concentric' castles in England and Wales – castles with walls built in rings around them.

1300s Rules for tournaments, like no striking below the belt. Also a scoring system to decide the winner in a friendly combat.

1315 Switzerland. Swiss foot soldiers use long-handled hooked knives called halberds to pull down and butcher charging knights on horses.

1320s Cannon first used in battle. Feeble things. No one worries too much about them ... yet!

1331 Switzerland. A tournament

injures many ladies when their stand collapses! Worse … as they try to free themselves peasants pinch their jewels.

1327 Edward II comes to the English throne. Tournaments become more colourful with bright costumes and great parades. By now knights are wearing complete suits of 'plate' armour instead of chain mail. (No, not dinner plates, stupid.)

1337 Start of 'The Hundred Years War' between England and France. A chance for knights to have some real battles.

1346 France. At the Battle of Crécy English archers stuff French knights. The power of the knight in battle is disappearing.

1347 Edward III of England holds a tournament at Windsor and gets the idea for a new group of knights: Knights of the Order of the Garter. (These knights will really have to pull their socks up.)

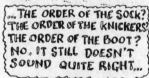

1358 Torchlit jousting in Bristol … 600 years before the first floodlit football match! And some castles in Britain and Holland are being built of brick!

1415 The Battle of Agincourt. English archers and horse soldiers defeat heavily-armoured French. The power of the knight is weakened again.

1429 France has its own Order of

Knights now: The Order of the Golden Fleece. (Popular with ram-raiders.)

1464 Mighty Bamburgh Castle on the Scottish border is captured using just two cannon. The power of the castle is disappearing.

1515 The Field of the Cloth of Gold tournament held in France. Henry VIII is the star even though rain stops play most days.

Late 1500s Knights with lances no longer so important in battles. Tournaments too are fading in popularity. The great days of the knight are over.

1621 Last of the old tournaments in England.

Dark knights

Super chivalry

'Chivalry' meant a set of rules that knights tried to stick to. They didn't *have* to, but they believed they were better knights if they did.

For example, you might be winning a fight against another knight when he lowers his sword and says, 'I surrender!' A *good* knight would say, 'That was a jolly good fight, old chap. Come back to my castle for a bite to eat and we'll chat about your ransom.' A *bad* knight would say, 'You're dog-meat – in a tin!' then poke his enemy in the eye with his sword.

Nowadays most sports have some chivalry in them – if an opponent is injured in soccer then you might kick the ball off the field to stop the game so he or she can get medical treatment. There is nothing in the *rules* that says you have to. You do it to be chivalrous and most people call it 'sporting'.

These knights were fighting to the death – yet they had rules of chivalry as if it was a boxing match: 'I'll do my best to punch you senseless – but if you fall down I won't kick your head in to finish you off … and I expect the same from you.'

Some rules of chivalry are still used today in battle – enemies usually allow stretcher-bearers with red-cross arm bands on to a battlefield to pick up the wounded. These rules didn't just come from the battlefield. A lot of the rules came from *stories* about knights. Adventure stories turned into poems and sung in castle halls.

The most famous stories were about French warriors who fought against the Saracens in Spain. Of course the heroes were good fighters and brave and true to their king. But what made them knights was their 'chivalry'. The way they *behaved*.

Because they behaved like real nerds.

Take the French super-heroes Oliver and Roland. Listen to this story and decide who is the knight and who is just a brave soldier.

Pull up a bearskin rug, sit in front of the crackling castle fire and listen to this modern version of the ancient poem…

Roland and Oliver – men behaving sadly

King Charles the Great, a mighty king (some called
   him Charlemagne)
Had mighty armies: men with strength but
   very little brain.
The greatest of his fighting knights was Roland,
   proud and brave,
And here's the tale of his last fight that brought him
   to his grave.

The armies of King Charles had been down south to
   fight in Spain,
But trouble back in France had made them head for
   home again.
Then Ganelon, the stepdad of great Roland (what
   a rat!),
He told the king, 'We'll leave the hero and his friends
   till last.

'My Roland he can guard our backs as we march
   home from Spain.'
And Charles said, 'What a good idea! Spain might
   attack again!'
Proud Roland said, 'I'll do the job, you go ahead
   my king.
I'll follow on with Oliver, don't worry 'bout a thing.'

17

But little did they know the wicked Ganelon had gone
And told the Spanish of the plan to leave his own
stepson.
The Spanish and their armies let King Charles and
his men go.
Then hid in mountains near the narrow pass at
Ronccvaux.

So Roland with his Oliver (he sometimes called
him Olly)
Rode through the pass, all dark and cold, and yet
they felt quite jolly
Until they reached a narrow part and then the foe
appeared.
But Roland (being a hero) was quite pleased and
not afeared.

Young Olly snatched at Roland's horn and said, 'Give
it a blow!
King Charles will hear. He'll hurry back.' But Roland
just said, 'No!
I'm not afraid of any man. I will not blow my horn.
This army of the Spanish I will treat with simple
scorn!'

But Olly argued, 'There's not just *one* great army
here.
There's more behind and right and left. There's *five*
at least I fear.'

But Roland scoffed, 'My sword shall run with their
blood, red and hot.
We'll stand and face them to the death!' And Olly
said, 'You what?'

'A curse on any man who shows some fear!' brave
Roland cried,
And Olly said, 'I'm not *afraid* … I just don't want
to *die*.'
And so the two great friends rode out to fight their
greatest battle.
The Spanish fell to right and left. They slaughtered
men like cattle.

And Olly said, 'Here, Roland! Why not give your
horn a blow?'
But Roland said, 'We've killed one army. Now just
four to go!'
And army number two were carved up into little
pieces,
Three and four were terrified and died like
shivering meeces.

But when they got to army five they found the foes
were tough.
(Apart from which poor Roland's men were
running out of puff.)
The Spanish fighters cut the heroes down in pools
of blood,
And Olly sighed, 'Oh, Roland! This idea was not
so good.

'We could have called for help, we could have lived
to serve the king.'
But Roland said that heroes didn't do such easy
things.
'A hero's just a man and he must do what he must
do!'
But Olly shook his head, he knew his friend had
some loose screw.

So Roland went down fighting but, my friends, you
should not cry:
Although his bleeding body's gone his name will
never die.
He faced the foe and never, ever gave up on the fight.
For Roland showed the world just what it means to be
a knight.

Poor Olly died as well, of course, although he was so
smart.
While traitor Ganelon was tied to horses … torn
apart.
And Roland's wife died too, for his death drove her
round the bend.
The one who lived to tell the tale was sad King
Charles. The end.

SNIFFLE...

Roland became the perfect idea of a knight. His story was sung around the world. All knights wanted to be like him and there are still people who think that this is the way to fight.

Rule one of chivalry became, 'Fight no matter how hopeless the battle; die rather than run away.' Five hundred years after Roland, knights were still dying this way. Knights like Louis Robessart...

Louis' last stand

Daily Standard
LATE KNIGHT EXTRA

STILL ONLY 20 GROATS!

IT'S GOOD NIGHT TO A GOOD KNIGHT

KNIGHT OF GARTER GALLANT BUT GUTTED

The spirit of Roland is not dead ... but Louis Robessart is. Knight of the Garter Robessart (43) died heroically yesterday fighting impossible odds.

In the Anglo-French wars in northern France he was ambushed by a huge force of the evil enemy. Amazingly, our brave battler butchered hundreds and his mighty men drove the attacking army off. Edward Edwinson (15), squire to Robessart, said last night, 'He fought like Roland himself even though we were outnumbered a hundred to one ... well, maybe three to one. They were coming at us from every direction. I wasn't half scared! But Sir Louis made them run! They shot off like greasy pudding off a plate.'

Robessart was resting his men after the fight when he received news that the enemy were on their way back. This time they had another army of fresh fighters to back them up.

His leading commander asked if they should retreat to a nearby friendly castle. Robessart is reported to have said, 'Retreat? I don't know the meaning of the word!' Edward Edwinson says he tried to explain that it means 'run away' but Robessart would not listen.

The young squires like Edwinson and the foot soldiers were sent to the safety of the castle and Robessart turned to face the fierce foe with just a small band of knights around him. Of course, he was soon cut down. Lady Robessart is said to be very cut up by the news. 'But not as cut up as Sir Louis,' her maid said.

The fearless fighter's body has been recovered. It will be boiled to remove the flesh and the bones carried home to a champion's grave.

The king, Henry VI, said, 'The war has been going on for 93 years now and men are already calling it the Hundred Years War. With a few more brave men like Robessart it wouldn't last another 93 minutes!' No one is sure if he means we'll win or get massacred.

But you couldn't always find a battle to fight in. There had to be other things you could do to prove you were a true knight.

Knightly rules

Knights had more rules than your school. It's true they didn't have *daft* rules like, 'Don't run in the corridor,' or 'Don't let the tyres down on the headteacher's car.' But they did have rules … some of which you could still follow today!

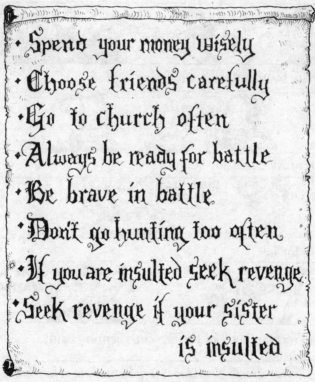

- Spend your money wisely
- Choose friends carefully
- Go to church often
- Always be ready for battle
- Be brave in battle
- Don't go hunting too often
- If you are insulted seek revenge
- Seek revenge if your sister is insulted

There are some rules the knights believed in that we still have today. We have sayings like, 'Never kick a man when he is down.' How ridiculous! Who says you shouldn't kick a man when he's down? What better time *is* there to kick a man? If you kick him when he's standing then he might just kick you back.

But, above all, a knight should be a *lover*.

Crazy courtly love

A knight without a woman-friend was like a bun without a beefburger. He was empty.

A woman-friend was someone who gave his life a real *purpose*. He could…

- fight for her

- write beautiful poetry for her

- do brave deeds for her

- die for her.

As a German book of the eleventh century said…

> *A young knight should woo a noble woman. He should knock at her door until it opens. He talks with her by her fireside for she will want to talk away the sorrows of her heart.*

Please note 1: Cuddling is allowed but it must be kept secret. Public cuddling is not on. If the woman is unmarried then her dad will get upset with you. If the woman *is* married then her husband will get upset with you.

Please note 2: A married woman is best. She probably only married some lord as part of a deal about her land. She will be bored and lonely.

Please note 3: Noble women only. A knight who falls in love with a peasant – even a high class peasant who washes her feet – is a disgrace. It is best if the woman is even more noble than the knight. Loving a queen is probably best of all … unless you get caught, of course.

The perfect lover

Jaufre Rudel was often seen as the perfect example of a knightly lover. And he only got to see his love one time … but *what* a time.

Jaufre was in love with the great Countess of Tripoli. She was said to be one of the most beautiful women in the world. Jaufre wouldn't know exactly *how* beautiful because he never saw the woman. This didn't stop him sending her endless love poems.

At last she invited him to meet her. He walked into her castle, took one look at her beautiful face and was overcome. He collapsed into her arms and died on the spot.

He was the perfect lover. The only man ever to have been killed by beauty.

Every knight knew Jaufre's story and every knight believed *he* was that much in love with *his* lady.

BUT...

This book is a *horrible* history. And the horribly sad truth is Jaufre did NOT die in the arms of the Countess of Tripoli. He lived on until he died of old age.

Knight school

Why not train your very own knight? After all, you never know when a dragon might land in your back garden and start eating the lawnmower! What would you do if you didn't have a knight?

Here's how you can make one. You can always keep him in a cupboard till you need him...

1 Take a seven-year-old boy. (In this modern age of equality you could take a girl if you really wanted to. Unfortunately girls tend to be a bit too intelligent for this sort of work.)

2 Send the boy away from his home, to the home of some other knight. (No, he *can't* take his mummy with him.)

26

3 Make your boy spend the next five years running errands, serving at meal times and doing other jobs in the house. He'll be known as a 'page'. (Boys who try to iron your baked beans or microwave the cat should be sacked.)

4 When he reaches about 14 years old he can become a 'squire' and act as the personal assistant to a knight. At the same time he will learn knightly skills – using and caring for weapons, armour and horses. (Polishing chain mail is hard work. And polishing a horse is even harder.)

5 When he's an expert fighter aged between 18 and 21 he's probably ready to be knighted. He has to be 'dubbed' a knight. (In the early days, this meant being struck on the back of the neck or the shoulder with the flat of a sword. Only another knight could do this to a squire. Try not to use the edge of a sword – the blood makes a right mess of the armour.)

6 From the 1100s onwards the squire would have to go through a church ceremony to become a knight. The night before the ceremony your squire is stripped by other squires and given a bath. (Cold water is good enough for a squire. If he is too wimpy to have a cold bath then sack him and start again.)

7 Dress your squire in a white tunic and a scarlet cloak, with black shoes and socks. A white belt goes around his waist.

8 Your squire goes to the local church, places his weapons on the altar and spends the whole night praying. (A squire who can't stay awake a night can't stay awake a knight. Sack him, because you want sleepless knights, don't you?)

9 Next morning a priest will bless his sword and give it to the squire. The squire will then pass the sword on to the knight who is going to dub him. The squire kneels and the knight will tap the sword on the squire's shoulder. He will then give the sword *back* to the new knight. (This sword is going back and forth a bit, isn't it? It might be a good idea to keep it on a bit of elastic.)

10 You now have a knight. Send him off to kill dragons or rescue ladies in trouble. (While you can have a good knight out!)

Did you know…?
Some squires from poor families could not afford to buy their weapons and become knights. They stayed squires all of their lives!

Hare today, tomorrow knight!

Not everyone was knighted in a special ceremony. Knights could be created on a battlefield. Lords would often dub squires just before they went into fight with the words, 'Be thou a knight.'

In 1388 the English army faced the French army at Vironfosse. Neither side was ready for a fight. Then, at noon, a hare ran across the field in front of the French.

French knights began to climb on their horses and gather their weapons for a hare hunt. The English thought they were about to start an attack so young men were quickly knighted. The Earl of Hainault made 14 new knights in five minutes. But the battle never happened. The 14 knights became known as the Knights of the Hare.

Did you know…?
Normans believed only a knight could make a knight but Hereward, an English rebel, went to be dubbed by a priest. He fought so bravely against William the Conqueror that he was forgiven for being a rebel! Other rebels got the chop … and I don't mean a lamb chop.

The great garter
These days the monarch of the United Kingdom can make someone a knight in a very special club – a Knight of the 'Order of the Garter'. (A garter used to be a piece of elastic that Boy Scouts used to keep their socks up. But in the Middle Ages women used ribbons tied round their legs to keep their stockings up. Elastic hadn't been invented, of course.)

King Edward III decided to hold a Round Table Tournament at Windsor and create an Order of the Round Table. Then something happened to change his mind…

And that's the way it's stayed till this day. Members of the Order of the Garter have the words 'Shame on those who think this is shameful' on their badge – except it is written in medieval French: *Honi soit qui mal y pense.*

But is the story *true*? Historians used to be very snobbish about the story of the Countess and the garter. 'Nice little story for the school kids,' they smirked, 'but it never really happened.' *Now* they're not so sure. Some historians think there's a lot of truth in it.

None of them are *horrible* historians, of course. If they were they wouldn't ask daft questions like, 'Is it true? Did it really happen?' *Horrible* historians, like you and me, would ask, 'What would have happened if it was her knickers that fell on the floor? Would Ed have picked them up and put them on? And would the House of Lords today have 25 members of the Order of the Knickers? Would their motto be *Honi soit qui mal y pants*?' (Shame on those who have shameful knickers.)

Well … no, actually, because in the days of Edward III people didn't wear any knickers. But what else could she have dropped?

A snotty handkerchief?

Odd Orders

These clubs for knights were called 'Orders' and were a bit like the Brownies for girls – you all had the same badges, the same ideas and you did fun things together ... like half killing each other in play-fights. (In this the knights could be nearly as vicious as the Brownies!)

If the Queen won't make you one of her 25 Knights of the Garter then make up your own Order and knight your friends. To give you some idea here are a few other Orders from Europe...

The Order of the Golden Fleece, founded 1429

A French copy-cat called Philip the Good didn't want a garter, so he founded his own Order, the Order of the Golden Fleece. There is no story of him dancing with a golden sheep so the Order of the Golden Fleece is pretty boring ... unless you would care to  make up a story? The members wear a golden sheep around their neck. (No, a *model* sheep, not a dead ram, you fool.)

The Order of the Elephant, founded 1492

And how would you explain Danish knights having an 'Order of the Elephant'? Maybe this is for people who never forget! Or maybe it's for people with a thick skin. Or for people who spend the weekend tearing down trees with their noses. Luckily they don't have to wear an elephant round their necks.

33

The Order of the Thistle, founded 1687

The Scottish 'Order of the Thistle' is for 16 people and the Royal Family. They have a nice Latin motto suitable for teachers, football hooligans and rottweiler dogs: *Nemo me impune lacessit*. Of course you don't need *me* to tell you what *that* means ... but I will anyway. It means 'No one hurts me and gets away with it'.

The Order of the Bath, founded between 1399 and 1413

This British Order was almost forgotten until George I dug it up and dusted it off in 1725. The motto is *Tria juncta in uno*, which as you know means 'Three in One'. Three *what* in one? Three men in the bath? Must be a pretty big bath! And in 1970 the Queen allowed women into the order. She must believe in mixed bathing. Would you want to get in the water after they'd been in it?

So what Order would you like to invent?

The avengers

Knights had a thing about ladies in trouble. They went out to fight for an unhappy woman even after she was dead!

In 1286 the Duke of Bavaria found that knightly revenge can go beyond the grave...

34

Wilful Norman women

William the Conqueror took his knights to England in 1066 but they had to leave their wives behind. The victorious William rewarded his knights with gifts of land. This caused a problem for the knights. Should they stay and enjoy their new land in England? Or should they go back to their wives in Normandy?

A historian called Ordericus reported that in 1068 the women knew *exactly* what the men should do...

> *Some of the Norman women were so furious that they sent endless messages to their husbands. The messages said that if the husbands didn't return at once they would choose new men for themselves. The knights were confused. They knew that if they left their king and their comrades in an enemy country they would be called cowards, deserters and traitors. On the other hand they did not want the disgrace of their wives leaving them for other men.*

What would *you* have done in their position?

Some, like Humphrey de Tilleul, decided to return home. He was commander of the new Norman castle at Hastings but he gave up his job to go back to his wife. The Saxons' swords had failed to drive him back to Normandy – Mrs de Tilleul's letter succeeded.

Ordericus didn't seem to approve much of strong women. He told another story of a powerful woman who came to a nasty end...

> *Ivri Castle is cleverly built and strong. It was built by Alberde, the wife of the Count of Bayeux. This Alberde hired a brilliant architect called Lanfred to design the castle. When it was finished she had Lanfred beheaded so he couldn't build another castle like it anywhere else. But Alberde was too proud. She tried to have her own husband thrown from the castle but she failed. He had her put to death for this and Lanfred was avenged.*

You see, it wasn't only knights and soldiers who died in castles!

Troubadour tales

Where did knights get their ideas from? Who told them it was a brave thing to wander round rescuing ladies in trouble, killing dragons or looking for a fabulous church treasure called the Holy Grail?

Singers told them. Singers who chanted long poems in the castle halls and told tales of heroes like Roland. But the most popular hero in England was Saint George. He is the patron saint of England to this day. Almost everyone knows the story of Saint George killing a dragon ... and almost everyone is wrong!

Saint George did *not* kill a dragon. Here is the true story. Tell the truth to your teachers with this truly terrific troubadour tale...

George and the Dragon

The poor people of Palestine were panicked! A dragon had moved into a cool cave in the hills and sat there smoking like a damp fire.

'He'll have to go,' the king said. 'Kill him!'

So his knights charged up the hill on their horses … then charged down again but twice as fast.

'Did you kill him?' the king asked.

'Kill him? He nearly killed us!' the sad soldiers said sorrowfully. 'Seems he wants a sacrifice.'

'So, send some sheep,' the king sniffed.

Well, the dragon ate the sheep gladly and greedily … then sent for some more. It was feasting on sheep faster than the farmers could fatten them.

'I have heard that dragons like children,' the queen said.

'How sweet,' the king said.

'I mean they like to *eat* them,' she snapped.

'Not so sweet,' the king croaked.

'But he can last for one whole week upon a single child. That's cheaper than sheep at a dozen a day,' the cruel queen crooned.

And so the coward king passed a law. Every child was given a number. On Friday mornings one number was drawn out of a hat. This lottery for lads and lasses chose the luckless losers. Every week a child was taken and tied to a tree outside the dragon's cave.

And that was that. Week after week the woeful parents watched their children get chomped and chewed by the crunching creature. Until, one Friday, the king asked, 'Who's the lucky family this time?'

Shaking servants trembled to tell him but, in the end, one said, 'You are.'

'What was that? We don't have a child in the lottery!' the queen said quickly.

'The princess has a number,' the servant said. 'The princess insisted. She said that it was only fair. The princess was number 13, and today she won ... I mean lost!'

The queen was quaking with anger. 'Go and get her back!' she screamed at her husband.

'Sorry, dear, I can't do that,' the cringing king said.

'Why not? Are you scared?'

'No ... I'm terrified! I'll tell you what. We'll find a hero brave enough to go to battle with the beast,' the king suggested.

'Then be quick,' the queen hissed.

So a message went around the city asking for someone brave enough to risk a roasting to beat the brute and pinch the poor princess. That's when a stranger to the city, George, stepped forward. 'I will go, your highness,' brave George said.

'Good lad!' the king and queen cried. 'Here, son, take the royal sword.'

'I need no sword,' the young man said. 'I'll go with God ... and he's much better than a wicked weapon. I'll go unarmed!' he said and marched off up the hill.

'What a hero,' said the king. 'Such a pity that he's potty.'

But George was armed with courage and he reached the cave in time to see the petrified princess ... alive. 'I'm saved!' the princess cried, then noticed that the knight had no sword, no shield and no armour on. 'Pity that he's potty,' the princess wailed. Just then the dragon dragged his body from the cave. He looked at George and blinked.

The knight walked up to him and said, 'You foolish flying lizard! Do you not know that no one likes a bullying beast?'

The dragon growled a startled growl.

'You're all alone up here in this damp cave. Do you know why?' the young George asked.

The dragon shook his scaly head.

'Because you go around eating these charming children.'

'That's right! You tell him!' cheered the princess (thinking George was not so potty after all and even rather handsome).

'Now you go down into the meadows,' George went on. 'There you'll find some nice rich grass. Eating good green grass beats eating poor pathetic people.'

'And there are no bones in grass to get stuck in your throat!' the princess put in quickly.

The dragon nodded and he let the young knight lead him from the hillside down into the meadows. In the city people goggled at the sight of a vegetarian dragon.

'How did you do that?' they asked.

The young man answered, 'Jesus Christ said you must love your enemy.'

'Who's this Jesus Christ?' the people said.

George then told them all about the Christian faith. Within a week the city built a church and all its people prayed to Christ.

Of course, the fame of George spread far and wide and he became a saint. The man who beat a dragon – not with a sword, but with the words of love and reason.

The knightly challenge

Would you make a good knight? It's more than just being able to ride a horse and swing a sword. You have to know how to *behave*. If there was a written exam in knighthood, would you pass it?

1 Erneis d'Orleans is a traitor. You meet him in the cathedral at the coronation of your king Louis. What do you do?
a) Hack him to death with your sword.
b) Punch him in the head.
c) Let him go.

2 When it came to winning the love of a woman, knights were worried about competition from priests. (Priests were not *supposed* to have girlfriends, you understand, but some naughty ones did!) You agree with a French knight-poet called Guilhem, who suggested that a woman who loved a priest should...
a) Become a nun.
b) Have her head shaved like a monk.
c) Be burned to death.

3 Knights should go hunting from time to time so they can practise their skills in riding and using weapons. You agree with Raimon Llull's book written in the late

1200s that says you should hunt bears, lions and...
a) Rabbits.

b) Dragons.

c) Peasants.

4 King Edward I of England has set up a tournament to give you a bit of practice and he will be fighting in it. It would be a bad idea to kill the king so you agree to use a sword made out of what?
a) Rubber.
b) Blunt steel.
c) Whalebone.

5 During the First Crusade you are besieging Ascalon with more than a thousand soldiers. A gap appears in the wall. Your band of fifty knights has three choices. Which do you vote for?
a) Forty knights will rush into the city and ten can hold back the rest of your own army, so the forty get the glory.
b) Send foot soldiers and archers in first then lead your fifty men into the city.

c) Fifty knights rush into the city as soon as the foot soldiers are ready to follow.

6 You are the king of England and in 1274 you have entered a tournament in France. In the mêlée the Duke of Chalons fights his way towards you and tries to wrestle you off your horse. That's cheating! What do you do?
a) Wrestle back and try to throw him off his horse.
b) Call your knights to tear this cheating lord off your neck.
c) Break free and refuse to fight any more.

7 You are the knight errant Ulrich von Liechtenstein. (A knight errant believes his duty is to go wandering through Europe looking for good deeds to do.) You get a message saying a lady is surprised to see that you have a particular finger. She thought you had lost the finger fighting in a tournament for her. What do you do?

a) Cut off a peasant's finger and send it to the lady.
b) Cut off your own finger and send it to her.
c) Have a model of the finger made from solid gold and send it to her.

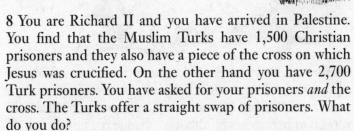

A FINGER OF FUDGE WOULD HAVE BEEN ENOUGH

8 You are Richard II and you have arrived in Palestine. You find that the Muslim Turks have 1,500 Christian prisoners and they also have a piece of the cross on which Jesus was crucified. On the other hand you have 2,700 Turk prisoners. You have asked for your prisoners *and* the cross. The Turks offer a straight swap of prisoners. What do you do?
a) Swap 1,500 Turks for the 1,500 Christians – but keep 1,200 Turks until the cross is returned.
b) Offer 2,700 Turks in exchange for 1,200 Christians, then offer 20,000 gold pieces for the cross.

c) Tell the Turks they can keep the cross and the 1,200 Christians. Butcher the 2,700 Turk prisoners.

9 You are the Earl of Suffolk. In a battle you are captured by a squire. You are horrified to discover that he is not a knight and it is a disgrace. What do you do to the squire?
a) Pay him to keep quiet.

b) Knight him there and then.

c) Kill him.

10 You are Bernard de Cahuzac and you are having an argument with the abbot of your local monastery. You have a small army of knights to back you up. What will you do to persuade the abbot to change his mind?
a) Burn down the monastery.
b) Lock him away and feed him bread and water till he agrees.
c) Cut the hands and feet off his monks.

Answers: **1b)** There's nothing wrong with killing a traitor, even in a church, but you should not spill blood on holy ground. French knight Guillaume d'Orange killed Erneis with a blow of his fist. Clearly Guillaume is not a blood Orange.

2c) Priests were not allowed to marry ... but they could be terrible flirts. And they spent a lot of time hanging around the noble ladies. Any woman who falls for a priest should be burned to set an example to other women.

3a) Knights only hunted dragons in stories. In real life, Llull said rabbits made for good hunting. A man in a can against a poor little bunny does not make such a good story. You might read about Saint George and the dragon but you won't read about King Arthur and the rabbit pie.

4c) Rubber hasn't been discovered yet, you dummy, so go to the bottom of the class if you said **a)**. Edward's 38 knights in the 1278 tournament had whalebone swords, 'armour' made from boiled leather – hard but light – and wooden shields. Clever Ed. He remembered his first tournament 20 years before where two knights were killed and another brain-damaged. He saved the sharp steel and hot blood for the battlefields of Scotland and Wales.

45

5a) Gerald of Ridfort went for glory. He led forty knights into the gap while the rest of his group held back the rest of his own army. The forty would get all the glory. *That's* knighthood for you. That's also pretty stupid. The forty got graves, not glory, when they were massacred. The soldiers who could have saved them and won the battle were just a spear's throw away outside the walls.

6a) King Edward wrestled back and threw the Duke on to the ground. The French knights were furious and wanted bloody revenge. English foot soldiers watching the mêlée aimed their arrows at the French, who were forced to cool down. From then on there was a rule that knights should not lay hands on an opponent – a lance, an axe or a sword, but not a hand!

7b) Ulrich was as nutty a knight as you could ever wish to meet. He is said to have cut off his finger for the honour of the lady. It's just as well the lady didn't hear he'd lost his head!

8c) Richard had the Turk prisoners killed with swords and spears. Of course, the Turks then massacred the Christian prisoners – they beheaded them. Richard did not consider there was anything wrong with killing Turks because Turks were not Christian. The Pope said it was all right for knights to kill non-Christians. The Christian prisoners who were beheaded may have had different ideas!

9b) Many knights believed they should only be captured by another knight. It was simply a matter of a knight putting a hand on a man's shoulder and saying, 'I knight you.' If a peasant was knighted in this way then there was a big fuss and the *peasant* would be punished. Even if he hadn't asked to be knighted!

10c) Not all knights were kind, generous and noble. Some, like Bernard, were simply bullies who used their power to get their own way. Of course, knights who followed the rules of chivalry would *not* have approved of Big Bernie!

Did you know…?
By the end of the Middle Ages a full suit of armour could cost up to £50,000 in today's money. Knights were usually rich lords because only rich lords could afford that sort of cash.

Terrific tournaments

Imagine walking to school. You reach a crossroads and there is the school bully. He stops everyone who walks past and says, 'I want to fight you!'

What would you do?

Say, 'Yes,' and spend the rest of the day dripping nose-blood over your books? Or say, 'No,' and be called a cowardy custard?

That's how tournaments started. Knights wanted fights. When they didn't get them they went out looking for them. So they stood at crossroads and challenged passing horsemen to a friendly battle.

Then, in the early 1060s, a French knight called Geoffrey de Preuilly organized these challenges into 'tournaments'. He practically invented a new sport. This is an extremely dangerous thing to do and you should never attempt this without your parents' permission.

In modern times the man who invented the sport of 'jogging' died while out jogging.

And what do you think happened to Geoffrey who invented tournaments? That's right. He died fighting in a tournament!

Horrible Histories health warning: Inventing a sport can damage your health.

Knights also used tournaments to practise their skills. This is like the school boxing champion standing at the crossroads and saying, 'I'm fighting in a school boxing match tonight. Let me punch your head in. It'll be good practice for me and I will win for the glory of our school.' Of course you would say, 'Yes.'

Wouldn't you?

SEEMS FAIR ENOUGH TO ME...

PAF!

Did you know...?

Tournaments were extremely popular and in 1140 the whole of Lincoln went to see the one being held there. The city guards also went along, and the Earl of Chester was able to attack the town and capture it ... with only *three* soldiers!

Mad mêlées

Early tournaments were usually known as 'mêlées'. A sort of free-for-all. Companies of knights would split up into two teams with their lords as team captains. There could be two hundred knights on each team.

The field of play would be several square kilometres and include fields, rivers and woods.

The sport we call 'boxing' takes *fist-fighting* and turns it into a game. But the idea is still to flatten your opponent. The difference is you have a referee to stop you killing him or her.

Tournaments took *war* and turned it into a game. The aim was still to capture an opposing knight and hold him to ransom. There were no referees or judges at first but there were 'safe areas' where a battered knight would be allowed to escape and rest.

What do *you* imagine the rules were?

Tick the rules you would agree with…

	Yes	No
1. Do not gang up in a group to attack another knight	☐	☐
2. Do not attack a knight who has lost some important armour	☐	☐
3. Do not use bows, arrows or cross bows	☐	☐
4. Do not hide and ambush opponents	☐	☐
5. Do not touch a knight in a safe area	☐	☐
6. Do not attack a knight who has lost his horse	☐	☐
7. Do not attack a knight from behind	☐	☐
8. Do not attack a knight waving a white flag	☐	☐
9. Do not strike below the belt with the sword	☐	☐
10. Do not try to kill another knight	☐	☐

How did you score?

Count your ticks.

7 – 10 ticks: You are a wimp. Forget about becoming a knight and take up basket-weaving instead.

3 – 6 ticks: Feeble. You would not last very long in a mêlée.

2 ticks: You are a knight ... *if* you ticked the *correct* two rules, number 5 and number 10. Knights in a safe area could not be touched and the aim was not to actually *kill* an opponent ... though many did die accidentally.

There were *no other rules*! Knights *did* attack un-horsed or disarmed knights who had lost their armour. They often joined into small gangs to attack a single knight and they would use any weapons they had – including crossbows. There were *no* foul blows and there was no white flag for surrender if the going got too tough. Mêlées were extremely rough games. *Almost* as rough as Year 9 girls' hockey.

Sometimes the knights got a bit upset and the fun-fight turned into a real battle with knights going for the kill – *exactly* like Year 9 girls' hockey!

Jolly jousting

As well as mêlée tournaments there were jousts. A man in a can with a lance trying to knock another man in a can off his horse.

51

In a 1216 tournament the French knights fought against the English knights using padded jackets instead of armour and lightweight lances instead of battle lances. This was so no one would be seriously hurt and it showed the tournament was 'friendly'. English Baron Geoffrey de Mandeville was killed. Some friends!

Mêlées were for the knights to enjoy and practise their battle skills. But jousts were for spectators.

Women could come and watch their lover (or their favourite knight) as he jousted. Sadly a woman could also be the prize! A German knight Waltmann von Setenstete said he was taking a beautiful young woman to Merseburg on a certain day. If any knight could beat him in a joust then the winner took Setenstete's armour and his weapons … and the young woman! Knights came from far and wide but Setenstete beat them all and the young woman was his.

AND THIS IS THE THIRD PRIZE: KEN

(Please note: Offering a young woman as a prize is disgraceful BUT … you could set up a sack race and offer your nasty little sister as a prize. Then deliberately lose to the ugliest challenger! That'll teach her to be Daddy's pet!)

Did you know…?
A knight could have an assistant, his squire, carry fresh weapons to him in the jousting area. But the squires sometimes got carried away and started using the weapons on the opposing squires. A new rule was invented. It said that any squire carrying a sword into the fighting area had to *hold it by the point*! Ouch!

Top ten tournament tips

If mêlées had only two rules then it was easy to cheat. Jousts had more rules, but it was still possible to trick the referee and cheat to win.

Of course, it was a huge disgrace to be caught cheating. Knights agreed it was better to lose with honour than to win with a trick. But you're not a knight and you can be a bit underhand if you want to. So, if you ever find yourself in a mêlée or a joust, then here are a few hints on how to succeed without actually cheating. Some villainous knights actually used these dodges…

1 Don't join in the mêlée at the start. Wait for the others to tire themselves out and then go in and grab a few exhausted knights. Philip of Flanders used this trick a lot … until someone tried the same trick on him and beat him!

2 Grab a wounded knight *after* the mêlée has finished and the knights are on their way back to dinner. William Marshal of England did this when a knight fell off his horse and broke a leg when riding home. Wily Willy captured him and demanded a ransom.

3 Have your armour made so you can be screwed onto your saddle! Knights who did this didn't fall off. Opposing knights got very angry at this trick, though. In the 1300s it was banned. In the 1400s Lord Wells accused a knight

of being screwed to his saddle. Lord Wells was wrong and had to grovel and say, 'Sorry!'

4 If you are supposed to be fighting with blunted lances, just take a sharp one into the fight. In 1290 Duke Ludwig of Bavaria died when a sharp lance pierced his throat armour. What a pain in the neck for Ludwig!

5 Have special armour made. A metal glove (gauntlet) that locks itself around a lance keeps it steady and makes it easier to hit the target. Another rule was added to make this illegal – if you were caught.

6 In a foot fight with axes, simply drop your axe and rush at your opponent. As he raises his axe to strike, draw your dagger and stab him under the arm. In a 1408 tournament a knight tried this on his deadly enemy – this was not a

fight for fun for them – but the king managed to stop him just in time. Others were not so lucky.

7 Use a lance that's longer and thicker than everyone else's! Bohemian knights did this in 1310 and they were unbeatable. Everyone refused to fight them ... so they fought each other instead!

8 In later tournaments you scored points by breaking your lance against your opponent's shield as you charged towards one another. The knight breaking the most lances was declared the winner. The trick is to have your lance made with a tip as frail as a glass butterfly and they'll break every time!

9 Catch your opponent asleep. In 1242 the Earl of Atholl knocked Walter Biset off his horse in a tournament.

55

Walter waited till darkest night fell, then crept into the Earl's tent and murdered him.

10 Have your opponent beaten up. A gang of squires with wooden clubs can jump on an opponent as he is on his way to the tournament. With a few broken ribs, legs and head he will not fight nearly so well.

Did you know…?

By the 1300s a curious idea came into the tournaments. Winners were losers and losers were winners. Here's how: the more times you were knocked off your horse and climbed back on, the braver you were. So if you were knocked off ten times and got back on ten times you were incredibly brave – if you were never knocked off then you hadn't proved your courage.

Sadly this idea is no longer popular. If it was then a British football team would win the World Cup, a Blackpool donkey would win the Grand National and my granny would win the National Lottery.

Pole poking for peasants

Jousting was more entertaining than a mêlée because it was usually one against one. A knight could really show off in a joust – in a mêlée he'd be lost in the crowd.

The peasants (like you and me) could go and watch the fighting knights but we wouldn't get a seat in the stands. We could always crawl *under* the stand … but this could be dangerous when the stand collapsed.

In Germany peasants actually held their own jousts and

tried to copy the knights. The knights hated these peasant tournaments but that probably made them even more fun for the people of the town!

Why don't you upset a knight or two and hold a Pole Poking contest which peasants found so pleasant? You could get together with a few friends and try to understand the excitement by playing to the same rules as the jousters.

You need
At least four people.
A space about 20 metres long and 4 metres wide with a rope separating it into two strips.
A few lances made from newspaper rolled from the corners and into a point at one end. All lances must be the same length.
A few shields about half a metre across – these can be painted with your favourite symbols and colours. (Please note: you can use your family coat of arms if you happen to be from a noble family.)
Swimming goggles (so no one is hit in the eye).

Rules
Two people are the horses and two are the knights. The knights mount the horses piggy back.

The mounted knights stand at either end of the rope.
At a given signal (like some beautiful maiden dropping a
handkerchief) the knights lower their lances and hold
their shields across their chests in their left hand.
They charge at one another and aim to strike the
opponent's shield with their lance.

Scoring

Around the year 1465 the Earl of Worcester came up with
a scoring system which you can still use today.

Knock your opponent off his or her horse: 5 points.

Break (or bend) the tip of your lance: 1 point.

Hit your opponent's horse with your lance: lose 1 point.

Winning

Ride three times against your opponent and keep the score.
Change round so horses become riders, then joust again.
Keep a league table and see who scores the highest.

Prizes

After everyone has fought everyone else the knights go off for a bath. Then they are awarded a cuddle from their lady. (Women riders, of course, get a cuddle from their lord. Horses get a cuddle from everyone and a sugar lump or two.)

Extra rules

You can make helmets with a 'crest' on top. The crest could be a card circle with a sign of your family on top. For example, if your name is Smith you could have a picture of a smith's hammer; if your name is Hill you could have a picture of Mount Everest; if your name is Scott you have a map of Scotland and if your name is Ramsbottom ... you'd probably be better off with a blank disc.

The Earl of Worcester gave five points for knights who hit this crest on the top of the helmet.

You can also make your own armour – but make it from cardboard or your 'horse' will end up bandy-legged.

Did you know...?

When there weren't enough knights to entertain the nobles they might arrange for some townspeople to have a fight. Two men from Ghent in northern Europe took part in a wrestling match. They wore shorts and greased their bodies so there would be no unfair gripping. Then they wrestled in the town square. Lords and ladies of Ghent took their places in stands to watch, just as they would for a joust. The fight ended when one of the men died. It was a contest as crude and violent as the Roman gladiators fought a thousand years before.

Round tables

As tournaments became more organized they grew into events called 'Round Tables'. Everyone knows the story of King Arthur and his Round Table knights. No one is quite sure who the real Arthur was – or if he ever really existed – but knights saw him as a good story to copy. So they...

- sat at a round table where everyone was equal. Before there had been a separate 'High' table for the king and his most powerful friends
- wandered around the world as 'knight errants' – looking for good causes to fight for and ladies to help

- took part in tournaments dressed as King Arthur's knights (though King Arthur would never have jousted with lances)
- organized 'Round Table' events – the first was in Cyprus in 1223 – with jousting and other sports.

If you want your own Round Table event then try some of the games the knights played. These included...

Casting the Stone
Competitors take it in turns to stand on a mark, pick up a large stone and throw it as far as they can. The one who throws it furthest wins.

You may recognize this as the modern sport of Shotputting. And the groovy Greeks played this two thousand years before the knights, of course.

(If you are too feeble to Cast the Stone then try something smaller and call it Putting the Pebble.)

Throwing the Lance

Competitors stand behind a mark. They pick up a lance and throw it. The place the point lands is marked. The furthest throw is the winner.

Again, you'll recognize this as the modern sport of Javelin.

(If you are too much of a wimp to Throw the Lance then challenge your weedy friends to Putting the Pencil.)

Potty prizes

Tournaments were about winning prizes. If you went to a fairground today you could throw darts or fire air rifles to win a cuddly panda or a china dog. Tournament prizes were a bit richer ... and more unusual.

A tournament in 1263 in Germany took place around a tree with gold and silver leaves. Break an opponent's spear and you get a silver leaf, knock him off his horse and you get a gold leaf. (Prizes you wouldn't want to *leave*?)

Winning a woman was rare but you could earn the following...

- 1216, London: the prize is a bear ... not much use unless you want to become a bear-back rider.

- 1350s, France: a golden thorn ... can you see the point?
- 1406, Italy: a silver lion and a velvet cap ... but what would a lion want with a cap?

- 1330, France: a golden vulture ... but could you afford the golden bird seed to feed it on?
- 1406, Italy: a helmet with a silver dragon's head, two golden wings and lots of red, white and green feathers ... would you be tickled if you won that?

• 1350s, Germany: a pair of talking parrots ... one for each shoulder?

At least some of these prizes seem worth winning. At the end of some tournaments there was a ladies' sprint race. They ran 'as far as a man can throw a stone' towards a table. On the table was their prize. A piece of cloth!

Did you know...?

Henry V was a great believer in chivalry. He believed a knight should not be killed if it could be helped. And a knight should *never* be killed by a peasant!

Henry's favourite groom was a peasant and, in a siege at Montereau, the young groom accidentally killed a knight. Henry could have rewarded the groom for his courage in battle. Instead he had him hanged for killing a man of a higher rank! Not pleasant for a peasant.

Cheerless churches

The Church thought it was fine to massacre millions of people who weren't Christian, but they didn't like tournaments where knights hurt one another for fun!

In 1130 a church law said:

The church bans all of these detestable markets and fairs where knights meet to show off their strength and courage. At these meetings men are often killed and their souls are in danger of going to Hell. If any man is killed at such a contest then he will not be allowed a church burial.

So there! Get yourself killed in a tournament and you won't be buried in a churchyard. But this didn't stop most knights. The truth is, they didn't *expect* to be killed so they weren't too worried about the Church's threat!

King Richard I (the Lionheart) tried to get round the Church's ban by selling tournament 'licences' in 1194. (He said the church would agree to his well-organized punch-ups.) He created five official tournament fields in England.

Knights expected to end the day's jousting by having a bath, a rest and a cuddle from a lady. One priest called Thomas of Cantimpre warned that the knights would be disappointed. He told the story of what happened when one group of knights ignored a Church request to stop fighting…

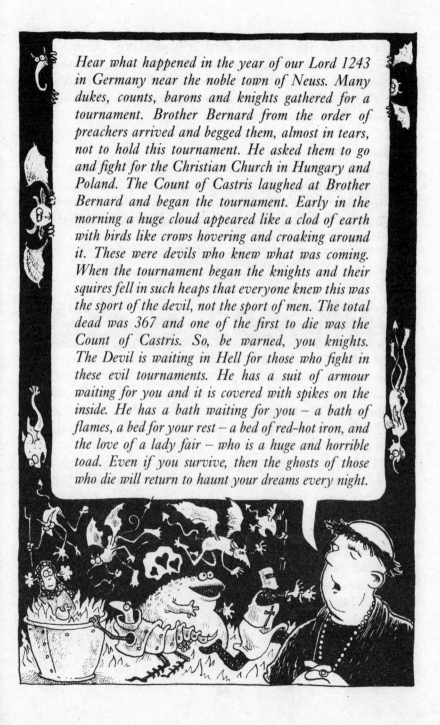

Hear what happened in the year of our Lord 1243 in Germany near the noble town of Neuss. Many dukes, counts, barons and knights gathered for a tournament. Brother Bernard from the order of preachers arrived and begged them, almost in tears, not to hold this tournament. He asked them to go and fight for the Christian Church in Hungary and Poland. The Count of Castris laughed at Brother Bernard and began the tournament. Early in the morning a huge cloud appeared like a clod of earth with birds like crows hovering and croaking around it. These were devils who knew what was coming. When the tournament began the knights and their squires fell in such heaps that everyone knew this was the sport of the devil, not the sport of men. The total dead was 367 and one of the first to die was the Count of Castris. So, be warned, you knights. The Devil is waiting in Hell for those who fight in these evil tournaments. He has a suit of armour waiting for you and it is covered with spikes on the inside. He has a bath waiting for you – a bath of flames, a bed for your rest – a bed of red-hot iron, and the love of a lady fair – who is a huge and horrible toad. Even if you survive, then the ghosts of those who die will return to haunt your dreams every night.

The truth is that 42 men died at Neuss, not Thomas's 367. He was wrong about that. So maybe he was also wrong about the red-hot, iron bed and the cuddly toad.

The Church finally gave up trying to stop knights from having their sport.

Horrible Hastings

William the Conqueror was encouraged by the Pope to conquer England. The Norman army carried a banner from the Pope and England was one of the first countries to be the target of a 'Crusade' when William invaded in 1066.

At the end of the Battle of Hastings William climbed to the top of Senlac Hill and planted the Pope's banner. But first he had to clear away the corpses of the Saxon defenders. (The banner probably said something Christian like 'Love thy neighbour ... but kill him if the Pope tells you to.')

The Normans had knights on horses but they weren't very sporting like the later knights. They saw the English King Harold was wounded with an arrow in the eye and started carving their way through his bodyguard to finish him off. They were screaming their war cry *Dex aie*, which means 'God's help'.

God must have been in a pretty vicious mood that day because four Norman knights reached Harold at the same time. They didn't say, 'After you, Jacques,' or, 'I say, Harold, would you like to get that arrow out of your eye before we challenge you to a fair fight?' They certainly didn't say, 'Four on one's not fair!'

The Bishop of Amiens described what happened next...

> *The first Norman knight split Harold's chest, driving the point of his sword through the king's shield. The gushing torrent of blood drenched the earth. The second knight struck off his head below the helmet and the third stabbed the inside of his belly with a lance. The fourth cut off his leg and carried it away.*

That really is making a good job of it.

But William the Conqueror was a bit more sporting. When he reached Harold's body bits he found a knight called Ivo chopping away at the dead king. William was so disgusted that he threw Ivo out of the army in disgrace.

Horrible heraldry

Knights had to wear colours to show which side they were fighting on. It's the same idea as football strips, really. At one tournament, for example, the Whites fought against the Colours.

But each knight also had his own 'family' colours. This told your enemy who you were and in a real battle that was important. He could then decide if you were rich enough to ransom – or so poor you might as well be killed. In 1073 knights did not usually wear family colours and it nearly cost a famous life.

William the Conqueror was at war with his son, Robert – trying to teach the lad a lesson, the way dads often do. Robert attacked William's forces and pulled a knight to the ground. Robert raised his sword for the kill and, with his other hand tore off the knight's helmet. That's when he recognized his father! He didn't really want to kill his own father but almost had by accident.

Soon afterwards, families started wearing some sort of sign – the Angevin family wore a sprig of the plant broom on their helmets, for example. Others painted a sign or a coloured design on their shield.

If another family had the same colours then there was trouble. In the 1300s the Grosvenor family had a blue shield with a wide gold band across it. The Scrope family had the same shield. The argument about who could have the colours went on for years. And it was important to the families as well as to their enemies. After all, you didn't want to grapple with a Grosvenor when you meant to scrap with a Scrope, did you?

The arguments were sorted out by the College of Heralds who kept a record of every family's colours and designs – the family 'coat of arms'. They kept their records in French, so the Scrope/Grosvenor colours were *azure à bend or*. That's 'blue with band of gold'.

The idea was that knights should gather together at their leader's banner – the banners weren't just pretty flags to wave for the television cameras. They were very important in battle. And in a tournament they were just like football strips at a modern match – the colours let the crowds see who was who. You could cheer for your favourites.

Did you know…?
A German knight called Max Walther went into tournaments with an unusual crest on top of his helmet. It was a spike that held three sausages!

Rotten ransoms

Before the English fought the French in the Battle of Crécy in 1346, knights weren't often killed in battle … unless it was an accident. They were far too valuable alive. If you captured a knight then you could sell him back to his family for a fortune.

Knights didn't invent the idea of ransoms. They were around in AD 679 when an English warrior called Imma was captured and held in chains. But by some miracle the chains fell off every time his enemies tried to fasten them on. He promised to go away and find the ransom money and return as a prisoner if he couldn't find it!

But ransoms didn't become really popular till after William the Conqueror. (He preferred to lock prisoners away for life.) By the end of the 1100s ransoms were much more common.

On the other hand, in some desperate battles a commander would order the prisoners to be killed. At the 1214 Battle of Bouivines in France the soldiers used a special three-edged dagger on the knights. It could force its way into the chinks in the armour. At Aljubarota, knightly prisoners were killed and the reporter on the battle said it was a sad thing. He didn't mean it was sad that so many knights *died* ... it was sad that the English knights lost 400,000 francs in ransom money!

Cruel Crusades

Crazy Christians

Blame Gregory the Great! Early Christians believed that war was evil and Christians shouldn't fight.

Then Gregory became Pope in AD 590 and said...

Of course, bishops were not allowed to spill blood – even heathen blood – so they went into battle with dirty great clubs called 'maces'. With a mace they could bash a non-Christian on the bonce and kill him without spilling a drop. Two Popes even went off to battle with their armies.

A new Christian belief grew: 'Love thy neighbour ... but you may need to batter him over the head with a stick if he doesn't have the same beliefs as you.'

When knights came along five hundred years after Greg the Great they had a perfect excuse for fighting. It was a war against enemies of the Christian religion and it was known as a Crusade...

Terrible Turk talk

In 1095, Pope Urban II decided it was time the Christians took over Jerusalem. It was their Holy City and was full of Turks, who were Muslims. Unfortunately it was also a Holy City to the Muslims and they weren't going to give it up without a fight.

The Pope's priests needed men with swords to drive the Turks out of the city so he sent an invitation to knights to fight for their Christian church.

The Pope didn't send out letters asking for volunteers. He stood on a platform and announced that he wanted Christians to fight against the Turks. He then did the old warmaker's trick of telling people how rotten the enemy was. Urban said...

The Turks cut open the navels of Christians that they want to torment with a loathsome death. They tear out their organs and tie them to a stake. They drag their victims round the stake and flog them. They kill them as they lie flat on the ground with their entrails out. They tie some to posts and shoot them full of arrows. They order others to bare their necks and attack them with swords trying to see if they can cut off their heads with a single stroke.

72

And you thought your history teacher was tough!

Of course, the Pope didn't know what he was talking about. He was repeating stories that he'd heard. The stories were mostly lies and the Turks were no worse than the Christians. In fact his Christian soldiers went on to be a *lot* worse!

Anyway, the knights of Europe got the message. Appeals went to every corner. These weren't the words used but the general idea was this…

KNIGHTS

Are you bored, sitting at home with no one to kill and no adventure to stir your blood? Then here's how you can change your life – this life and the next one!

YOU CAN

+ Join a fun trip to faraway places
+ Make new friends all over Europe
+ Fight and kill non-Christians – without breaking the laws
+ Book yourself a seat in Heaven for when you die
+ Return home a hero to your family and your lady friends
+ Loot heathen homes and make your fortune

HOW?

+ Join the Holy Army. Wear a cross on your tunic. Travel to Jerusalem - without turning back. Drive out the Turks. Win glory and fame. Remember lads - God's on our side - you can't lose!

Of course, the Crusades could cause you one or two problems – you could get killed, wake up dead ... then find God was on the side of the Turks!

Meanwhile the peasants of Europe were also being encouraged to march to Jerusalem. A potty priest called Peter the Hermit was telling everyone that if enough pilgrims reached Jerusalem then Christ would return to Earth. The pathetic peasants believed him and set off.

They weren't an army – they were a rabble. There were a few knights among Peter's pilgrims but a lot of women and children too. The thieving, destructive mob overran every town they reached.

They finally walked into a Turkish ambush. A Turkish princess, Anna Comnena, wrote 15 history books in the early 1100s. She reported the bloody end of the Peasants' Crusade...

They gathered up the corpses of the dead. I wouldn't say they made a hill ... I'd say it was more like a mountain of great height and width. That's how great the mass of bones was.

The French knights were having a better time. They set about massacring people on the way to the Holy Land. The trouble was they were massacring *Christians* because they hadn't reached the Turkish lands yet. When they finally met the Turks they were trapped in a castle with no water and forced to surrender. They had a choice – become a Muslim or die.

Their leader, Rainald, became a Muslim. Many others chose to die.

Awful Antioch

By 1098 the strongest group of Crusaders, led by Bohimund, had reached the city of Antioch in the Holy Land. It had been a long hard road and even potty Peter the Hermit had tried to run away – the great knight Tancred dragged him back.

The Turks locked the gates and the Crusaders began a siege. It could have gone on for a long time. But the Crusaders didn't have time. An army was marching towards them from Mosul. They had to get into the city before these Turks arrived or they would be wiped out.

That's when God seems to have decided he was on the side of the Christians for a change. They had three bits of luck. Firstly, Bohimund heard from someone willing to help…

Dear Mr Bohimund Sir,
    Hello. You don't know me but I know you. You're that big blond knight what leads them Christians aint you. Let me introduce myself. My name is Firouz – but I don't want anyone to know I'm writing this so don't tell anyone who I am.
                                                                                    P.T.O.

75

I am an armour maker and could make you a lovely suit. But that's not why I'm writing. I'm writing because I am chief guard at the Tower of the Two Sisters at Antioch. It's a rotten job and your siege is starving me to death. I tried to hide some grain but my commander found it and he fined me. Miserable swine. I also caught him in the arms of my wife. Rotten dog. Anyway, I don't want much. Just my revenge. If I let you and your men in through my tower will you promise to kill him?

Yours truly
Firouz ...
(who will remain nameless)

Firouz betrayed Antioch and let the Crusaders in. Every Turkish man, woman and child (except Firouz) was murdered that night.

Twenty thousand Crusaders were inside the city – but they'd done such a good job that there was no food inside the place.

Then the Turkish army from Mosul arrived.

Now it was the Crusaders who were besieged. And starving. That's when they had their second bit of unusual luck…

THE ANTIOCH TIMES

14 TH JUNE 1098   **1 GROAT**

MIRACLE MAN SPOTS SPEAR

Crusaders in Antioch Cathedral today witnessed the greatest miracle of the century. Four days ago peasant Peter Bartholomew went to Crusader leaders and told them that a secret lay beneath the floor of Antioch Cathedral. It was the spear that pierced the side of Christ as he hung on the cross 1,098 years ago.

At first the leaders were unwilling to believe the peasant who is better known for drinking than praying. But Peter Bartholomew insisted that they dig up the Cathedral floor.

Today a crowd of several hundred watched as workers pulled up the ancient floor and dug into the sandy earth. When the pit was as deep as a man the workers were ordered to give up. That was when

Peter Bartholomew leapt dramatically into the pit wearing only his shirt. 'Pray, you Christians! Pray!' he cried. Minutes later he screamed and came up clutching an old iron spear.

'It's a miracle!' the Pope's man Adehmar said as he lifted the spear. 'It is a sign from God that we are blessed. We must attack the evil men of Mosul four days from now and God will grant us victory. In the meantime we

must show our holiness. We must fast.'

Since the soldiers in Antioch have no food anyway this is a strange request. But no one's arguing with a sign from Heaven. 'It's God's will,' Sir Bohimund said and that's the battle cry the Crusaders will be shouting when our brave lads go out to face the foe.

Peter Bartholomew has been promised a reward by Adehmar, if we survive the siege, and told he is sure of a place in Heaven.

The 'miracle' could have been a trick, set up by leaders desperate to get their men to fight. If they stayed in the city they would die. People were already eating leather and stewed tree bark.

Four days later the weak and pitiful Crusaders struggled out of Antioch to face certain death at the points of Egyptian swords. And that's when the third strange bit of luck happened.

An unnamed historian of the time wrote…

The army left the city with only one hundred living horses. Two hundred stayed behind with Duke Raymond who was too weak to walk. The men marched behind the Holy Spear while priests prayed aloud.

And suddenly there appeared from the mountains a countless army of men on white horses whose banners

> *were white. When our men saw this they did not understand but said it was a heavenly host led by Saint George himself. The priests called upon the living God and the soldiers charged.*
>
> *When the Turks saw the army they fled. Our men fell on their knees and gave thanks for the miracle of the Holy Spear that had saved them.*

In fact, the ghostly army was another Turkish army, enemies of the Mosul Army who'd come to attack them – no Saint George and no miracle … except that they arrived at just the right time!

As for Peter Bartholomew, within a month some Normans were calling him a fake. He agreed to prove he was a saint by carrying the spear through a fire. He ran through the fire … and was badly burned. (Some people say he was pushed back into it by his enemies!) Twelve days later he went off to collect his reward of a seat in Heaven.

Cannibal Crusaders

God (or someone) sent a plague to Antioch in July and the Pope's friend, Bishop le Puy, died of the disease. The Crusaders moved towards Jerusalem but stopped to capture the town of Maarrat from the Turks. Again they captured a city with no food. This time they didn't waste human life by a massacre of the Turks.

As one writer, Radulph of Caen, said...

> *Our troops boiled heathen adults in cooking pots, placed children on spits and ate them grilled.*

They wrote to the Pope and said sorry ... they asked if he'd forgive them since they'd only eaten char-grilled Turk-burgers as a last resort when they were really hungry. So that's all right. (Eating Christian-burgers would have been a sin.)

The Crusaders climbed over the walls of Jerusalem on 15 June 1099 – three years after they had set off from Europe.

As usual they massacred the Turks inside. This time they had an extra reason for cutting up the corpses. A lot of the Turks put their gold in their mouths when they fought against the Crusaders, so that the Crusaders couldn't get at it. When they were cornered they swallowed the gold like a human piggy bank. It did them no good. The Crusaders learned about the trick and took the money out the shortest way – through the front.

Pope Urban's Crusade had succeeded! News was sent back to Rome! And I'll bet you think Pope Urban II was dead pleased? No. He was quite simply plain *dead*. He went off to his heavenly home just two days before the news arrived.

When the Turks fought back, a Second Crusade set out to rescue the first lot. They failed. Then a Third Crusade with Richard the Lionheart tried again. Richard was up against tough Turk Saladin and, after a lot of bloodshed, he failed too. Lots of Turks and Christians died horrible deaths but their deaths did no good.

By 1291, not quite 200 years after the First Crusade, the Christians lost their last city in the Holy Land.

Did you know…?

The Turks could be as ruthless as the Christians. In 1119 crusader Count Robert was captured in battle and taken before the Atabeg of Damascus. The Atabeg drew his sword and cut off Robert's head. As if that wasn't cruel enough he threw the Crusader's body to the dogs but kept his skull. It was encrusted with jewels and used as a drinking cup!

Mad monks

When the First Crusade had captured Jerusalem they hadn't had much of a plan about what to do next. Pilgrims were still in danger on the road to Jerusalem, so a new group of knights were formed. They were monks who had a house near the Temple in Jerusalem, so they became known as the Templars.

This was like a club for big boys with some weird rules. They weren't like the jolly jousting knights back in Europe. These boys were Serious (with a capital 'S').

1 As in any army, there were rules against going off without permission ... but the Templars had a rule that said they must leave the Temple House by the *front door*. This was to stop anyone sneaking off and enjoying himself.

2 Other knights fought in tournaments ... Templars were banned.

3 Other knights hunted deer and wild boars ... Templars were only allowed to hunt one type of animal, the lion.

4 They were not allowed any pleasures like gambling, heavy drinking or going out with women. (It's surprising there wasn't a rule against breathing.)

5 Punishments could be cruel. They could be made slaves in a monastery for a year or even locked away in a dungeon for the rest of their lives.

6 Some of these monks were quite mad. They thought it was good to starve themselves from time to time. But they could take this a bit far and starve themselves till they were weak. This is *not* a good idea if you are going into battle. In 1216 the Bishop of Acre preached to the Templars and told this story…

My friends, let me tell you about a Templar who was more interested in fasting than fighting. Our friend ate nothing but bread and water for a week before a great battle against the Turks. When the time came to put on his armour he was fastened into it by a friend. With the stiff armour his legs were straight. This is just as well, otherwise he would have fallen over.

Our tottering Templar was helped into the saddle by four knights and managed to sit up straight. His horse walked to the battle and somehow he stayed on. When he reached the battlefield he trotted towards the enemy and his bones rattled inside the armour like nails in a tin pail.

An enemy rode up to this Templar and swung a sword at him. The sword clattered harmlessly on his armour, but the blow knocked him clean off his horse. A friend helped him rise to his shaking legs and mount the waiting horse.

Again he rode forward. This time an arrow hit his breastplate and bounced off. But the tap was enough to knock him into the dust again.

Again his friend helped him up. But this time the angry friend said, 'If you fall off again, Sir Bread-and-water, you can find someone else to pick you up!'

Templar terror

The Templars held lots of castles and wealth in the Holy Land. They also began lending money because they had so much to spare.

They never paid ransoms. Their Grand Master was captured in 1177 and the Turks asked for a ransom. The Templars refused and the Grand Master died in prison.

Of course, sooner or later, someone came along who wanted all of that Templar money.

That someone was King Philip IV of France…

84

Fighting facts

Pester your parents. They want you to do well at school and get a good report. Tell them you need to practise your knowledge of warfare in the Middle Ages and torture them with these questions...

True or false...?

1 When a knight in armour fell off his horse, he couldn't get up again and fight.

2 Stairways in castle towers go up clockwise.

3 Richard the Lionheart had an unbreakable sword.

4 Besieged castles kept in touch with friends by using carrier pigeons.

5 Knights didn't always charge on horseback. Sometimes they crept up on enemy tents to murder them in their sleep.

6 Swords were polished with a cloth dipped in vinegar.

7 If a baby was going to grow up to be a knight then his first mouthful of food should be from a silver spoon.

8 A Crusader would share his tent with his horse.

9 One group of Crusaders were led by a goose.

10 Once archers had used up their arrows they had to hide behind the knights.

Answers: **1** False. Most armour allowed the knight to move easily. A knight could turn a somersault and vault on to his horse. With just a breastplate a knight could climb the underside of a ladder – very difficult but a safer way to reach the top of a castle wall!

2 True. If someone is chasing you up a castle tower then it's easier for a right-handed swordsman to back up the spiral stairs. A right-handed attacker would find it difficult. BUT some castles, like Caerphilly in Wales, have a couple of stairways that go anti-clockwise. If you found you were fighting to get *into* your own tower then you would choose one of those.

3 False. King Richard set off on the Third Crusade and took a hawk from a peasant – he said hawks should be used only by lords. A mob of peasants surrounded him and Richard slapped one man with the flat sword blade. It snapped. Richard just about escaped with his life. Swords were blunt and brittle things for bashing, not slicing.

4 True. The Crusaders learned this trick from the Turks. Messages were fastened to pigeons' tails or under their wings, not their legs. There are several stories of pigeons landing in the wrong camp and giving away secrets or having their messages switched so enemies were tricked. In 1171 the Turks even had a pigeon relay system to carry news from one end of their empire to the other.

5 True. On 15 April 1291, for example, a group of Templar knights crept into a Turk camp. They seemed to forget that tents are usually held up by ropes. One knight tripped over a rope and fell head first into a ditch that the Turks used as a toilet. He drowned in the sewage. Yeuch! The rest of the force were captured and executed. Their heads were tied round the neck of a horse and presented to the Sultan next day. The Battle of Otterburn in England, 1388, also started with a night attack and ended with the English attackers blundering to defeat. They attacked the baggage train by mistake and missed the Scottish knights. It seems dark knights can get confused on dark nights.

6 True. The sword was kept in a scabbard but could still begin to lose its shine very quickly. A young squire would probably have the boring job of polishing swords and armour with vinegar. Chain mail was put in a sack with sand and vinegar in it, then shaken about till it was clean. (Note: this does not work on school blazers so don't try it.)

7 False. The first mouthful of food should be eaten from the tip of his father's sword if he was going to grow up to be a knight! Hopefully the father wouldn't have a shaky hand as the baby was fed, otherwise the baby might grow up to be a sword-swallower!

8 True. And some knights in the heat of the Holy Land made sure their horses had water before they did.

9 True. In 1095, when the First Crusade set off, one group of pilgrims found a goose that they thought was sent by God. They began to play Follow My Leader with it. When they ran out of food they probably played Eat My Leader.

10 False. The archers would also be armed with swords and some even had horses. Once their arrows were finished they would attack with other weapons.

Gory guns

Guns often get the blame for driving knights off the battlefield, but that's not really the case. The longbow and the pike did more damage before guns had been invented. The crossbow was banned by the Church in 1139 because it was so cruel and deadly! It could go clean though a knight and kill him. This was too easy and took all the 'sport' out of war.

The first guns and cannon were feeble things compared to the longbows, crossbows and the catapults the knights already had. During the Crusades Richard I used flint boulders in his catapults and these burst into splinters as they landed. One shot was said to have killed twelve Turks when it landed in Acre.

Cannon balls were not so deadly. And the guns were not so reliable. If a gunner had had to instruct a new recruit in Scotland in 1460 then he may have said something like this...

The grumbling gunner

Do you know how old I am, sonny? I'm thirty years old. And I just happen to be the oldest gunner in the Scottish army. In fact I could well be the oldest gunner in the world.

Why's that? Because this gunning lark is a dangerous job. Now don't look so worried, sonny, I'll take care of you. With any luck you'll live to be thirty years old too.

Now, when I was your age, things used to be a lot safer. We made our gunpowder with very coarse saltpetre. It burned nice and slowly, you understand. The trouble was it didn't give a lot of power. Sometimes a cannon ball hardly had the power to get out of the barrel. So what did we do? We started using *fine* saltpetre and *then* the fun started!

You see it caused a big explosion in the barrel. It blasted a cannon ball out faster than a sneeze. But if the cannon ball stuck in the barrel the explosion had nowhere to go. It blew the cannon apart!

You'd take the smouldering rope, touch it to the touch hole and 'Wham!' Fingers all over the place. We buried dozens of fingers – look, I lost a couple off my right hand myself! No, don't look so sickly, sonny, or you'll never make a gunner.

Anyway, my mates found my fingers and we gave them a decent Christian burial. I was one of the lucky ones. The unlucky ones lost a hand or an eye. Of course we learned our lesson. We started leaving a trail of gunpowder up to the touch hole. We lit the end then got a safe distance away before it burned down and set the cannon off. I haven't so much as singed an eyebrow since I started using a gunpowder trail.

But I was at Roxburgh Castle when the siege was on in 1460. You've heard about that, I suppose? You haven't? Well let me tell you. It was our job to punch a hole through the walls of the castle and King James II bought a cannon specially for us. It came all the way from Flanders and it was bound with metal hoops so the barrel couldn't split.

The old king was ever so proud of that cannon. He called it 'The Lion' … yes, it's a daft name. You know what lions do … they bite anyone who comes near them. Well, James wanted to see it in action. So we took it up to the walls of the castle and laid a long trail. I told his majesty, I said, 'When I light the powder trail then get your head down in this trench.'

He laughed. He had a lovely laugh, the old king. 'The Lion won't explode,' he said. 'It's the greatest cannon in the world! I want to see it fire and I want to see the walls crumble.'

'If you'll excuse me, sir, I'll light it and I'll duck in the trench,' I said.

'Go ahead,' he smiled. Did I tell you he had a lovely smile?

So I lit the powder trail. I heard the explosion and I saw the metal flying over my head. I waited a little while and raised my head. The king was lying there as peaceful as a sleeping baby. Except sleeping babies don't have a surprised look on their face. And sleeping babies don't have the top of their head sliced clean off.

Aye, the royal brains were decorating the turf that day. The Lion had bitten its master.

Now look, sonny, if you're going to be a gunner you'll have to be tougher than that … and don't go being sick over those new cannon balls, lad! Hey! You what? What do you mean you're going to ask to be transferred to the archers?

I don't know. Young lads today. Soft, I tell you. Soft! Softer than King James' head. At least, soft as it was when The Lion had finished with it.

Did you know…?
In 1450 Charles VII of France boasted, 'I have the greatest number of veuglaires, serpentines, crapaudines, culverines and ribaudequins that have ever been collected in the history of man.' He wasn't talking about musical instruments, satin jackets or pet rabbits. He was talking about the different types of guns his army had.

Battles and blood

Brilliant battlers

Knights did not spend all their lives posing on horses and having fun fights. Many knights had quite heroic lives. Here are some of the leading lancers and super swordsmen of the Middle Ages.

Name: William Marshal
Life: England, 1144–1219
Claim to fame: As a child he was captured by King Stephen. The king threatened to throw young William into his father's castle with a giant catapult unless his father surrendered. (His father *didn't* surrender, but William lived.)
Worst moment: He knocked Prince Richard

off his horse in a tournament. But a few days later the old king died and Richard became king. William Marshal was accused of trying to kill the new king. 'If I'd wanted to kill you then I could have done,' he shrugged, 'but I didn't.' Richard pardoned him. William once won a prize at a tournament but wasn't around to collect it. He was found in the blacksmith shop with his head on the anvil – his helmet was being bashed back into shape so he could get it off!

Name: Bertram du Guesclin
Life: France, 1320–1380
Claim to fame: When he became a knight he led an attack and climbed the walls of Melun alone to defeat the defenders and let his men into the city. He also rescued his younger brother from the English by offering to fight for him – he beat the English champion and won his brother's freedom.

Worst moment: Because he was an ugly child his parents treated him as a servant. He ran away from home and learned to fight by leading a gang of young men.

Name: Edward, The Black Prince
Life: England, 1330–1376
Claim to fame: Captured King John of France at the Battle of Poitiers then served the king at the victory feast. He said it was an honour to serve a great knight like King John. Prince Ed was a daring leader – at Najerilla in Spain he led his army round a mountain to

catch his enemy by surprise. It worked and the Prince's men massacred the opposition.

Worst moment: Caught a disease when at war in Spain and never really recovered. He was a tough character and often massacred people in towns he defeated. On his deathbed a bishop asked Prince Edward to forgive his enemies, as all good knights should. Ed clamped his mouth shut rather than agree … soon after he was a dead Ed.

4 Name: Ulrich of Liechtenstein
Life: Bavaria, 1200s
Claim to fame: Fell in love with his lady (he says) when he was just twelve years old. He then travelled round Europe as a knight errant and proved his love by fighting anyone. He dressed in a long blonde wig and a woman's dress – which is enough to put any opponent off! On his  'Venus Tour' (as he called it) he offered a gold ring to anyone who could defeat him. Anyone who beat him had to pay tribute to his lady and bow to the four corners of the earth. Ulrich claimed he had broken 307 spears.

Worst moment: Getting a ladder in his tights as he was about to joust. (Only joking, Ulrich!) He had to give away 271 rings so he can't have been that good a fighter.

5 Name: King Edward I
Life: England, 1239–1307
Claim to fame: Very keen on tournaments and on the legend of King Arthur. He brought a bit more law and order to tournaments: spectators were no longer allowed to carry weapons. Before this they often killed rival supporters! Ed used his jousting skills in real battles against the Welsh, the Scots and the French.

Worst moment: In his first tournaments in France he was beaten several times and lost a horse and armour each time. Later he became bored during a quiet half-hour in a battle. He challenged an enemy baron to a joust. Ed was doing well so the enemy baron tried to pull him off his horse. This was considered cheating so Ed's men joined in and massacred the opposition.

6 Name: Geoffrey of Bouillon
Life: France, 1100s
Claim to fame: At Antioch Geoff was challenged to a duel by a Turkish knight. They rode at each other and Geoff used his huge sword to chop through the Turk's waist. The top half of the Turk 'lay panting on the ground' while the bottom half went off at full speed on the horse! Another Turk was cut by one of Geoffrey's downward swipes; the

sword went through his head, through his body, cut through the saddle and into his horse.

Worst moment: At the siege of Rome he was the first to break through the walls. He was sweating terribly with the effort but instead of having a drink of water he

swallowed enormous amounts of wine. It brought on a fever that killed him.

7 Name: Baldwin
Life: France, 1058–1118
Claim to fame: As a leading Crusader he became the first Christian King of Jerusalem. He led a company of 200 knights in an attack against a Turkish army ... then found there were twenty

thousand of the enemy surrounding him! Most of them died, but Baldwin managed to get the fastest horse in town and galloped to safety in the hills.

Worst moment: At another Crusade battle he was left with just three other knights.

They decided that it would be wise to hide in a bed of reeds. The Turks didn't bother to go into the reed bed after them … they just set fire to the reeds. In fact the smoke screen helped him to escape but he was badly burned.

8 Name: Rodrigo de Bivar
Life: Spain, 1040–1099
Claim to fame: This great Spanish fighter was nicknamed El Cid – The Lord. He had a lion for a pet and was unbeatable in battles against the North African invaders, the Moors. It was said that in one battle he cut down 300 Moors personally.

Whenever the enemy saw him they ran away (though that could have been something to do with seeing his lion!).

Worst moment: Rod had a dream that he would die in 30 days. He ordered that after he had died his men should fasten his corpse to his war horse, so his body could lead his men into war one last time. The Moors heard that El Cid was dead – when they saw the body riding towards them they thought he'd risen from the dead and ran away. Who can blame them? The Spanish couldn't bear to bury him so they sat him on a throne for ten years before they put him underground!

Sometimes it's hard to be a hero. In the attack on Jerusalem the Crusaders only had one ladder to climb the walls. Everyone wanted to be a hero and be first up the ladder ... even though the Turkish army was waiting at the top! In the end Raimbaud Creton won the honour. He climbed the ladder to the top and placed a hand on the battlement. That hand was instantly cut off. The price you pay for being a hero is never being able to tie your own shoe laces again.

Did you know...?
Crusader Baldwin lay dying in Egypt but he didn't want to be buried in a Muslim land. He wanted to be taken back to Jerusalem where he had reigned as king. The trouble was that his body would go mouldy on the long journey, so he left instructions that he was to be preserved...

As soon as I die, I beg you to open my stomach with a knife, take out my insides, embalm my body with salt and spices and wrap it in a skin or cloths. In this way it may be taken back for a Christian funeral in Jerusalem and buried next to my brother's grave.

Egypt was a good place for him to die because he was actually asking to be made into a Middle Ages mummy! And who got the job of salting the body? The army cook, of course!

Nasty knights

Knights fought in tournaments for practice. It was practice for battles that they never fought! We've all seen knights on the cinema or television screen. They charge into the attack with banners waving and clash with the enemy knights. But that hardly ever happened in the real wars of the Middle Ages.

The truth was that wars were more about cutting off the enemy's supplies, burning the crops in their fields, and besieging their castles till they starved.

If you *did* happen to meet an enemy on an open field of battle then it was best if you *didn't* charge him. That's the best way to get beaten. Wait until he charges you. Eager knights who got carried away and charged first often lost a battle. In 1187, for example, Gerard of Ridfort attacked a large enemy force at Cresson. What a hero! A hundred and thirty knights set out to attack 7,000. Gerard returned with just *two*! A hero? Or a dummy?

You can see the problem, can't you? If you charge at the enemy the knights in your army are split up and it's hard for them to get back together for another charge. Each knight ends up on his own and is easier to pull off his horse. But some knights could fight alone if they were strong enough, vicious enough and skilled enough. When you met a knight like that it was better to go home and have a cup of tea while he massacred your mates.

Robert Guiscard was the sort of Norman knight you wouldn't want to meet in battle. One historian wrote...

> *Marvellous sword strokes were given on both sides. Here and there you could see human bodies split apart from the head downwards and horses cut in two along with their riders. Robert Guiscard saw his brother being attacked by the enemy and threw himself into the fight with fierce courage. He pushed his lance clean through his enemies, he lopped off their heads with his sword, with his strong hands he pole-axed them with frightful blows. Three times he was thrown from his horse and three times he gathered his strength and rode back into battle, spurred on by his rage. Burning with anger he cut off their hands and their feet. Here he would split a head open and the body with it; there he would rip open a belly and a chest; another man's ribs would be stabbed after cutting off his head. After the battle it was agreed that no one had struck mightier blows.*

Nice chap. His mother probably thought he was a lovely lad!

Wild women

Did you know...?
1 Not many people realize that women went on Crusades along with the men. The Second Crusade had women riding with the men and sitting astride their horses. The historian who wrote this was quite shocked at the idea!

2 Crusaders often took old women with them and these women had two main jobs. One was to wash their clothes and the other was to comb their hair and keep their heads free of lice. They were said to be 'better than monkeys'.

3 In the Third Crusade many women took part in the siege of Acre. They attacked the Turks with huge knives and brought Turkish heads, dripping with blood, back to their homes.

4 Women who followed the Crusades had the important job of keeping the men supplied with water. They took a great risk because if their army was defeated they would become slaves or corpses.

5 Women Crusaders helped in emergencies to defend their cities. One historian tells of a woman who was helping to build an earth wall when she was struck by a Turk javelin. As she died she begged to be buried in the earth wall. Her corpse, she said, would become part of the defences.

6 Women who stayed at home had the difficult task of running the home or the castle. At first they could object to their husbands going to war – marriage vows were very important. But in the thirteenth century Pope Innocent III said a Holy War was more important than a marriage. A woman could not stop her husband from going.

WELL ALL RIGHT THEN – BUT MAKE SURE YOU'RE BACK IN TIME FOR TEA

7 A woman whose husband went missing didn't always know if he was dead or alive. If he was dead she could marry again. If no one knew what had happened then lawyers could set a time limit. Some courts said a woman could marry if her husband had been missing for five years. But some said he had to have been gone one *hundred* years!

8 The most famous woman soldier, of course, was Joan of Arc. This French peasant girl heard voices that told her to put on armour and lead the French armies to victory over the English invaders. She had many surprising successes but was finally captured by the English.

9 The English could not execute a prisoner of war – it would not have been very sporting. So they said her voices weren't angels ... they were devils. Joan was *not* a saint ... she was a witch. What do you do with witches? Burn them. In 1421 the twenty-year-old heroine was burned at the stake.

10 The most unusual castle defence came from a woman. In 1461 Lady Knyvet was left to defend Buckingham Castle in Norfolk. She leaned out of a tower window and called down to her attackers, 'If you try to attack the castle then I shall defend it. I'd rather die defending it than give it up. My husband left me in charge and if I lose it then he'll kill me anyway!' The attacker, Sir Gilbert of Debenham, gave up and went away!

Letters from the front

Some battles were so important they changed the way knights fought in battle. From being unbeatable super-men they became tin-plated dummies to be knocked over and knifed.

Very few people, apart from monks, could write. Even kings like William the Conqueror never bothered to learn. That's a pity. If some of the soldiers had written down their experiences in the bloodiest of knights' battles then they'd have made horrible historical reading. They may have looked something like this…

Crécy, France. August 1346.

Dear Mum,

Just a line to let you know I'm safe. You probably heard about this awful battle here at Crécy. Battle, did I say? More like a massacre. Blood all over the place. I reckon the English only had 20,000 men to the French 40,000. We should have won easily! It was the usual plan. We would fire our crossbows at the English knights when they lined up, then our knights would charge at them and wipe them out. Easy.

The trouble was the English cheated. The knights didn't get ready to charge. They just stood there and waited for our French knights to charge! I could see that Black Prince lad standing there and I'll swear he was laughing!

Anyway, our French commanders sent us forward first with our crossbows, and that's when we had the first bit of bad luck. It started raining. Not drizzle but it was raining cats and dogs. That reminds me, Mum, I hope you're keeping my Tiddles well fed. I miss her.

So we plodge forward and try to shoot the knights down. What happens? Our bowstrings are wet and stretched. A cat can vomit further than our bolts could shoot. Not that it would make much difference. The sun came out and blinded us so we couldn't see the enemy anyway. And we were so short of crossbow bolts we wouldn't have done much damage.

And that's when the English really cheated. They had those longbows from Wales. They'd kept their bowstrings dry in the shower and they started firing at us. Longbows fire more arrows than crossbows - about one every ten seconds. They don't go as far as a crossbow but they don't half hurt. Naturally we turned and ran back.

Our knights were furious! They called us soldiers cowards and tried to charge towards the English lines. The problem was our crossbow men hadn't had time to get out of the way. So they chopped us to pieces to hack a way through. Our own knights killing us! The lads that survived were cross, I can tell you. In fact we were almost cheering when the longbows killed hundreds and hundreds of those vicious French knights. I was counting, Mum, and I can tell you they charged fifteen or sixteen times. They had to charge through a muddy swamp that the rain had left. If they got past the swamp and past the arrows then the English knights dragged them off their horses.

As for King John of Bohemia, what a hero! What an idiot. As you know he is stone blind. So he tied himself to a knight on either side and rode into the attack. I don't know what he was hoping to do. It was suicide.

Still, you can't feel too sorry for the old geezer. He paid a doctor to cure his blindness. When the doctor failed King John had him sewn into a sack and thrown in a river to drown.

But to get back to the battle. It was all over by nightfall. We had the charming job of bringing in the wounded and burying the dead. About 10,000 of them some reckon. The miserable English only had to bury about a hundred. It's all right for some. Of course, the burial job had its rewards. You can't bury a man with his purse or his jewels, can you? When I get home I may have some nice presents for you.

And talking of presents, I know what sort of gift I'd like. I want one of those big Welsh longbows. I lost my crossbow somewhere on the battlefield and I'll be happy if I never see it again.

Hope to get home soon, Mum. Don't forget to feed the cat.

Your loving son,

Ernest xxx

If the French made a mistake at Crécy then they made a bigger mistake at Poitiers, almost seventy years later. At Agincourt in 1415 a huge French force could have surrounded the little English army and starved them into surrender. Instead they decided to attack. But after the lesson of Crécy they decided their knights should go *on foot*!

The English army waited and cut the lumbering French knights down. The French didn't understand. You can *defend* a battle on foot but you can't *attack* that way!

The knights in armour were defeated by the archers and the fast-moving soldiers on horseback. Knights fought on in spectacular tournaments, but after Agincourt, they were never going to be lords of the battlefield again.

It wasn't the first time that armoured knights had been beaten in a battle. That probably happened in Scotland in 1297…

Stirling Bridge

Dear Ma,

You wouldn't believe it but we've beaten the English! Get the porridge in the pot, I'll be home soon.

Lovely Porridge

That English king wants to take over Scotland? He'll have to think again after today's glorious victory. And it was foot soldiers like me that defeated the high and mighty Englishmen in their shining armour.

Of course we didn't have many knights because King Edward of England has locked them all away. But the Scots' William Wallace is a clever leader - and we're the bravest soldiers on this Earth. They say the English had 10,000 men - twice as many as us. But clever Willie Wallace placed us at the end of Stirling Bridge. It's a narrow bridge and only two knights could get across it at a time. What did we do?

We let them cross – at least, most of them. Then we ran down the hill, kilts flying and throats raw with screaming, and we met them before they had a chance to get settled for a charge at us.

The English knights were lashing at us with battle-axes, maces and swords. But we had long spears and we knocked them off their mighty horses and stabbed them through the gaps in their armour. They lay on their backs and kicked like beetles.

That's when their commander panicked and he sent the rest of the knights rushing over the bridge. But there were too many, Ma! The bridge collapsed and they fell in the swampy water and drowned. And the ones who'd already crossed over couldn't get back. A knight in water's like a fly in porridge.

A few of their foot soldiers swam back to safety but the knights were butchered like sheep at a November fair.

I've a few bits of armour to show you, Ma, but Willie Wallace has the best prize. He has the corpse of King Edward's own treasurer, Hugh Cressingham. Wallace says he's going to make a sword belt out of the man's skin! I wish I had a sword belt like that.

Not that I'll need it. England will never dare attack the brave Scots again as long as Wallace lives. The lords have named him 'Guardian of Scotland'.

Make that porridge good and thick, Ma, for killing's

a hungry business.
   Your dear son,

TAM x

But Edward I took charge of the English army himself and set off for revenge against Wallace.

At Falkirk in 1298 the English knights charged at the Scottish spear men. The Scots stood shoulder to shoulder and the knights could not break through. It was another 'first'. The first time foot soldiers had stopped a charge by knights.

But that tightly packed block of spear men had one weakness ... they were a tightly packed target for the English archers. Once the arrows poured into the Scots, they 'fell like blossom in an orchard when the fruit has ripened. Their bodies covered the ground as thick as the snow in winter.' That's how a later historian described the massacre.

The second charge of the knights destroyed them.

Seven years later William Wallace was betrayed to the English. He was tried in London then hanged till he was half dead, cut open while still alive, beheaded and cut into quarters. His head 'decorated' Tower Bridge while the quarters of his body went on display on castle walls in Newcastle, Edinburgh, Berwick and Perth.

A sickening sign of what would happen to rebels against Edward.

Did you know…?

Many battles in the Middle Ages were decided by the archers and not the knights. Each side began the battle by filling the air with arrows. Every archer tried to keep six arrows in the air at a time!

One way of firing quickly was to have the arrows ready by sticking them in the ground, points down. Of course the arrow points picked up dirt this way. If an enemy survived an arrow wound then he could die of blood poisoning a few days later. The rule during the arrow attack – for both sides – was 'Don't look up!'

The archers used 'flight arrows' first. They had long shafts and travelled over 200 metres. Then as the enemy drew closer they used 'sheaf arrows' which were shorter and could 'punch' a hole through a knight's armour.

The worst job on the battlefield was being a 'retriever'. That's not a dog. It's a soldier whose job was to run onto the battlefield and grab any undamaged arrows from the ground. Very dangerous!

Horrible for horses

A knight's best friend was his horse. A brave, fast horse would be a great help in battles or in tournaments. Of course, you needed more than one horse. And you had to be careful not to lose in a tournament. Your opponent often took your horse and your armour as his prize.

Being a knight could be exciting, glamorous and win you great rewards ... being a knight's horse could be simply *horrible*. A knight who hit a horse in a tournament could be disqualified. This was no comfort to the horse that had a metre or two of wooden pole stuck in its chest.

Find the nearest Pony Club member in your school and shock them with these foul facts…

1 Sometimes horses were trained to fight with their hooves and teeth. This was great in a battle. The trouble was they started attacking their owners and the squires who were trying to look after them!

2 Foot soldiers found that the easiest way to bring down a charging knight was to bring down his horse. Arrows or poles with sharp blades (called 'pikes') were often aimed at the horse and not the rider.

3 In battle a defending army would often throw down 'caltraps'. These spiky metal stars would always land with a point turned upwards. The point would dig into the foot of a horse and make it run wild with pain.

4 Knights got wise to this and started putting armour on their horses. The weight of the knight, his armour and his horse's armour was huge. Then the horses were expected to gallop. (But knights' chargers did *not* look like cart horses, the way some

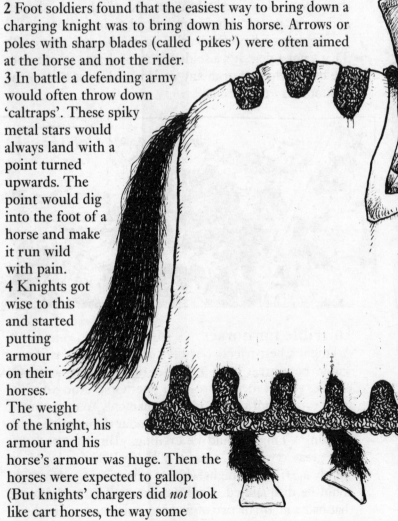

school books describe them. They were more like the horses used by fox-hunters today.)

5 Henry VIII went to France and took part in a tournament, called the Field of the Cloth of Gold, where he just had to be the star. One day he wore out his best horse and it was dead by nightfall.

6 Horses often had the lances of clumsy knights smashed into their chests as they charged in a tournament. The knight lost points for this – the horse often lost its life! One horse broke its neck as it crashed into the saddle of another horse. Barriers were placed between the charging riders, which helped to protect the horse … usually.

113

7 But in a 1443 tournament there were no barriers. Knights on large horses could batter knights on smaller horses by making sure their horses collided. But Galiot of Baltasar went further. He had spikes hidden under the cloths on the front of his horse. Any horse that crashed into his soon became, well, dog meat.[1]

8 Even dead horses were useful to an army. The mouldy corpse of a horse would be loaded into a catapult and fired over the walls of a castle. As it splattered inside the walls it would attract flies and germs like a railway station attracts anoraks. The French did this at the castle of Thin. (Nowadays this is known as 'germ warfare'.) Of course, you have to be careful not to fire fresh horse meat into a besieged castle. Then the defenders would say 'Thank-you' and feast on horse-burgers!

9 Dead horses were also used by King William II to fill up a ditch in front of Mayet castle so ladders had something to rest on. That is seriously sick … but other stories say a few peasants were also thrown into the ditch to fill in the gaps!

1 Gruesome Galiot was caught but not banned. He claimed that everyone in his home country of Spain fought with a spiked horse. Nobody believed the spiteful Spaniard.

The defenders were just as sick. They threw a rock at William – it missed him but splattered the man next to him. 'Ha!' the defenders cried. 'At least the king has got some fresh meat now!' Yeuch!

10 King Richard the Lionheart was chasing an enemy when the enemy turned to fight. The knight that faced Richard was the great champion William Marshal. Ooops! Richard realized that he'd forgotten to put his armour on. 'By the legs of God,' he cried. 'Do not kill me. I am not armed!' The sporting Marshal did not want to kill an unarmed man ... so he killed Richard's horse instead! What had dead Dobbin done to deserve it? Sometimes it was horrible being a horse.

Dingy castles

Sticks and stones

117

Cutter Whey Castle

No book on castles seems to be complete without a drawing to show the insides of a castle. But you can't see the insides of a castle from the outside – even Superman's X-ray eyes can't see through two to three metres of stone wall! So the artist *pretends* that the walls have been cut away.

But a Horrible History wouldn't do anything so cheap and cheating. Instead Horrible Histories sent the artist and a demolition gang to a castle and actually knocked down the walls so the artist could sketch the scene for you!

We chose Cutter Whey Castle, which is two miles to the west of Blackpool … at least it was. Shortly after the last sketch was made the castle fell down because we cut away a bit too much. (If you are ever walking on the beach at Blackpool you will find stones … these are almost certainly the remains of Cutter Whey Castle and proof that it did exist at one time.)

Cutter Whey Castle 1: before

WORKSHOPS Around inside of curtain wall. Heres a leather worker softening leather by trampling it in a mixture of water and doggy-Poo

CURTAIN WALL: To keep attackers out, and soldiers in.

I ALWAYS DID HAVE SMELLY FEET!

GATEHOUSE: Drawbridge at the front. Portcullis at the back. A Portcullis is a sort of grate

THIS IS A GRATE-HOUSE!

DUCK!

LATRINE SHAFT: Waste from the toilet drops through this hole into the moat. But beware: Enemies can try and crawl up here - if they're foolish enough (or Poo-lish enough)

120

Cutter Whey Castle 2: after we demolished a few walls

WARDROBE – A room for her ladyship's servants and her clothes.

SOLAR – The posh and cosy living room for his lordship

FANCY! SLEEPING IN A WARDROBE

KITCHEN TOWER Separate from the main hall because of the danger of fire. Of course food is cold by the time it reaches the table.

Dingy dumps

Castles were really *fun* places to live in. They didn't have the boring things that we have today ... but it has to be said, they were pretty dingy. They had...

- NO double glazing ... instead they had *draughts*. Shutters were put over the window spaces to keep out the cold but they didn't stop draughts. Tapestries were hung on the walls to stop the wind whistling round your neck, but it was still draughty. Ask your parents ... draughts are better than double-glazing sales people any day.

- NO toilets ... just *garderobes*. These little rooms jutted out from the castle walls and human waste dropped straight down into the moat below. (Ducks just had to ... duck!) If you sat on the garderobe seat a cold breeze would keep your bum cool. But at least there were no toilets for the school bully to stick your head down and flush.

- NO electric cookers ... just wood-burning ovens and open fires. Meat would turn on a spit over the fire and as the fat dripped down on to the flames the fire would spit back. (There was a lot of spitting going on in castles, what with the fires and the people at the dinner table.) The meat would be a bit burned on the outside and a bit raw on the inside. This meant that there was a good chance you'd get food poisoning, of course. But at least you wouldn't have caught mad cow disease (or mad chicken, mad pig, mad mutton or mad treacle-pudding disease, either).

• NO carpets ... just reeds that were scattered on the floor to mop up the grease you spilled. You could eat with your fingers and throw bones to the dogs. Of course, what went in one end of the dog came out of the other. You had to watch where you were putting your feet. But at least you didn't have your mother whingeing at you to 'Wipe your feet before you come in the house'. You'd probably have had to wipe your feet before you *left*!

• NO beds ... except for his lordship's. Peasants like you would just sleep on the reeds on the floor. They'd be greasy and smelly and full of fleas ... but then, so would you, so why worry? You would

have animal skins or rugs to keep you warm. But at least you won't have someone nagging you to make your bed.

- NO bathroom … just the odd swim in the river in summer to wash the lice and fleas off your body. Some fussy people had a bath filled with water that had been warmed over the fire. But at least you didn't have potty parents going on about washing behind your ears. (Have you ever asked them *why*? Nobody ever *sees* behind your ears!)

Castle characters

The lady and the lord

The constable

The jester

The butler

The farrier

I NOT ONLY MAKE SHOES FOR HORSES BUT I ALSO TREAT THEM WHEN THEY'RE SICK. I'LL VET YOU DIDN'T KNOW THAT!

The prisoner

THEY CALL ME AN 'OUBLIETTE'. THAT'S FRENCH FOR A FORGOTTEN PERSON — A PRISONER. AT LEAST, I MAY BE A PRISONER... I THINK I'VE FORGOTTEN...

The guard

CAW! I AM A WATCH-MAN AND ALL WATCH-MEN ARE NICKNAMED 'JIM CROW'! CAW! FANCY THAT! I AM ALSO PAID LESS THAN ANYBODY ELSE! CAW!

The gong farmer

I CLEAN OUT THE TOILET PITS. I WORK REALLY HARD BUT NOBODY SEEMS TO LIKE ME. THEY WON'T EVEN SHAKE HANDS WITH ME!

The castle cat

I CATCH THE ROTTEN RATS. MOST PEOPLE LIKE ME... BUT THERE'S A TRADER WHO SELLS FUR COATS AND I DON'T LIKE THE WAY HE LOOKS AT ME!

Did you know…?

If a pig is frightened before it dies then you get tough pork. But a happy pig gives you tender pork. So the castle butcher would make sure the pig was really, really happy … then bop it on the head with a hammer before it knew it was going to be the filling in a sausage!

So, things were a lot worse for some folk than for others, I think you'll agree, and worst of all for the gong farmer. But they all had to suffer life in these dingy, draughty, damp dumps. HOWEVER … they did have one thing that is sadly missing in the modern house. They had…

129

Dreadful dungeons

Imagine having your very own dungeon. A sort of playroom from Hell. Instead of toys you could fill it full of Middle Ages torture machines then invite your history teacher in to test them. Please note: History teachers are very keen on 'Living History' these days. They believe pupils should *experience* what it was like to live in the past. They take their class to some heritage site to live for a day as Vikings/Saxons/Tudors/Victorians chimpanzees or something. It looks good on the head teacher's report to the governors. 'Class 3C visited the Roman village of Boringium and spent a day living as slaves.' It is *always* cold, the food always tastes terrible, the clothes itch and the tasks you are given are always boring – making coil pots or sniffing herbs in the kitchen garden. So your teacher should really enjoy spending a Living History day 'experiencing' life in a dungeon or torture chamber.

130

One victim of the torture chamber in the Tower of London described the experience. He was a priest called John Gerard and in 1597 he was being accused of holding illegal Catholic services:

We went to the torture room in a kind of solemn procession, the guards walking ahead with lighted candles. The chamber was underground and dark, especially near the entrance. It was a huge, shadowy place and every device and instrument of human torture was there. They pointed out some of them to me and said I should have to sample them. Then they asked me again if I would confess. I said...

What would *you* say? What did John Gerard say?

Answer: John Gerard said, 'I cannot confess.' He was tortured and lived to write his story.

Terrible tortures

The Tower of London's dungeon was known as 'The Pit'. It was below the high-water mark so when the tide came in water flooded the floor and the rats scampered through to keep their feet dry. Chained prisoners got wet feet. But that was the least of their worries.

Just 13 years before Gerard went to the Tower,

Sir Thomas Smith, Elizabeth I's secretary, wrote:

> *Torture, which is used in other countries to make people confess, is not used in England. This country dislikes killing and spilling blood. We will not stand for beatings, slavery and cruel punishments.*

Sir Thomas was either a) very stupid or b) a liar.

Here are a few of the 'experiences' you can treat your teacher to:

1 *The Rack*

How it worked: The victim was laid on a wooden frame and ropes tied his or her hands and feet to a roller at each end. As the rollers were turned in opposite directions the prisoner was stretched.

Foul facts: Guy Fawkes confessed after a long brave fight against the Rack. He confessed at last but his stretched arms were so weak, the signature on his confession was just a scrawl. The first Rack was brought to the Tower of London by the Duke of Exeter. It was nicknamed 'The Duke of Exeter's Daughter' and prisoners put on the rack were said to be 'married to the Duke of Exeter's Daughter'.

Quick quote: The torturer in Tudor times was Thomas Norton. Norton stretched the priest Alexander Bryan. He boasted, 'I stretched him a foot longer than God made him.'

2 *The Boot*

How it worked: A piece of heavy wood was placed down each side of the prisoner's leg. Wedges were hammered in between the leg and the wood so that the leg was steadily crushed.

NO! WHEN I SAID I WANTED A PAIR OF BOOTS...

Foul facts: The Boot was often used on witch suspects in the 1590s. In 1596 Thomas Papley was kept in a Boot for eleven days and nights, without any clothes in a freezing cell. As if that wasn't enough, he was also whipped with birch twigs.

Quick quote: King James II was an especially nasty man, as Bishop Burnet reported: *When any man was tortured in the Boot it happened in front of the Council. Almost all of the councillors wanted to run away. But James was far from running away; in fact he watched carefully as if he was watching an experiment. Everyone who saw this got the impression that he was a man without a drop of mercy.*

3 *Skeffington's gyves*

How it worked: This was an iron hoop in two halves joined by a hinge. The prisoner, hands tied behind, knelt in one half while the torturer closed the second half shut. The prisoner was squeezed into a tight ball.

Foul facts: Leonard Skeffington was in charge of the Tower in the days of Henry VIII. This machine could be carried to the prisoner's cell and used there. It saved trips to the torture chamber.

Quick quote: In 1580 Thomas Coteham was crushed in Skeffington's gyves. A witness reported, *He bled considerably from the nose.*

4 *The Gauntlets*

How it worked: The prisoner stood on blocks of wood. His or her wrists were fastened in iron handcuffs to a beam above the head. One by one the blocks were removed till the prisoner was standing on tiptoe and finally swinging from the beam.

Foul facts: A priest was stood on steps and fastened into Gauntlets. The torturer then took away the steps. But the priest was so tall his toes touched the floor anyway! The torturer had to scrape away at the earth of the floor till the priest's feet had nothing left to rest on. After half an hour the priest's arms were so swollen he couldn't use them to feed himself. He had to have his food cut up and fed to him by servants.

Quick quote: Elizabeth I's torturer, Richard Topcliffe, seemed to enjoy his job of hunting down and torturing Catholic priests. Gauntlets were his favourite method of persuading the priests to talk. They would be forced to confess and give up their religious beliefs. But, as a witness said in 1586, *Only a man like Topcliffe could torture a man a second time after he has already been broken on the Rack, has confessed and has even given up his faith.*

5 *Thumbscrews*
How it worked: The victim's thumbs were placed under a metal bar. The bar was slowly screwed down so that it squeezed the fingernails.
Foul facts: Thumbscrews were first used as a sort of hand-cuff. Prisoners were lead around with a rope attached to the bar. In the 1400s they were called penny-winks. Later they were used to squeeze confessions out of prisoners.

Quick quote: A report of 1683 described a Scottish Thumbscrew torture that went wrong: *William Carstares suffered an hour of the agony of the torture but they screwed so hard they were unable to unfasten him. A blacksmith had to be sent for with his tools to remove them.*

The torturous tickle
Of course, there is just a chance that your teacher may not enjoy any of these tortures and may actually decide Living

135

History stops with you making coil pots in some cold castle courtyard. Never mind, here's a French torture they just may let you try. All you need are stocks and a goat. Yes, *stocks* and a *goat* ... not *socks* and a *coat*.

First the offender had their feet fastened in the stocks so that he or she couldn't move them. Then salt water was poured over the feet. A goat was brought into the cell. Goats love salt. The goat will begin to lick the soles of the prisoner's feet. When the salt is licked off then more salt water is added ... until the tickled victim screams for mercy. Please note: Do not use a teacher with smelly feet otherwise the goat may die.

The cruel tower

The cruellest execution at the Tower was probably that of a bear. The animal had killed a young girl so it was sentenced to death. The executioner could have killed it quickly and painlessly but instead he decided to have some sport. He put some of the Tower's zoo lions into the bear's cage. The lions were too afraid of the bear to attack it so that plan failed. In the end savage dogs were set on the creature. But which is the cruellest animal? The bear ... or the executioner?

It is said that in January 1816 a sentry was guarding the jewel house when he saw a dark shape coming up the stairs towards him. As it drew closer he could see it was a large bear! He lunged at it with his bayonet but the weapon went clean through the body without harming it.

The Keeper of the Crown Jewels, Mr Swifte, said the man was a brave and honest soldier. After reporting the phantom bear the soldier fell ill and died two days later. The bear's revenge that had taken about 500 years to arrive, perhaps?

Clever castles

Imagine that you are William the Conqueror. You know all about castles because the Normans are the best castle builders in Europe. You build a turf mound (called a *motte*) and a wooden wall around the top.

The problem is you are about to invade England and attack King Harold. What will you do after you beat him? You'll be in a foreign country, surrounded by English people who want to see you dead. What you will need is a castle. Where can you get a castle from quickly?

Then you have an idea. It's a nutty Norman plan but it might just work. What is it?

Answer: Take a castle with you! William had a castle do-it-yourself kit made in Normandy. He carried it over to England and joined it all together when he reached Hastings. Amazing but true.

Castle cwiz

Teachers don't know everything. They just *think* they do. So, find your nearest teacher and test their brain cells (*both* brain cells) with this cunning castle cwiz...

1 Early castles had walls of wooden stakes that were sharpened to points on top. Wooden castles were often attacked by fire. Defenders tried to stop the wooden walls from burning by doing what?
a) Training a castle fire brigade.
b) Soaking the walls with their toilet bowls.
c) Covering the walls with leather.

2 Castle walls had shelves on the outside so defenders could climb out and drop something on attackers' heads.

What did they usually drop?
a) Boiling oil.
b) Water.
c) Petrol.

3 In warfare both attackers and defenders used huge catapults to fire boulders. A rope was twisted and stretched like elastic, then released. But they didn't have rubber in the Middle Ages. So what were the ropes made from?
a) Human hair.
b) Cat gut.
c) Cows' tails.

4 The castle toilet was known as the 'garderobe' because it 'guarded robes' or cared for clothes. But why was a toilet thought to be a good place to keep clothes?
a) Because it was a smaller and warmer room than a bedroom.
b) Hanging clothes around the walls kept draughts off you.
c) The smell kept cloth-eating moths away.

5 The French word *malvoisin* means 'bad neighbour'. But what meaning did it have in a castle siege?
a) It was a knight who lived near your castle, often visited you and knew all the secret entrances. He was a 'bad neighbour' because he told your enemy your weak spots.

139

b) It was a tower that was filled with men and pushed up against the castle wall – it became a 'neighbour' to the wall. The men climbed out and attacked.

c) It was a type of bull, trained to charge anyone who tried to cross his field. If an enemy camped under your walls then you'd let out the *malvoisin* bulls and they'd chase away these unwanted neighbours.

6 What use was a tortoise to someone attacking a castle?
a) Tortoises were thrown into the castle gardens where they ate all the greenery and the castle defenders starved all the quicker.

b) 'Tortoise' was the name given to a 'shell' that attackers carried over their backs as they tried to dig at the foot of a castle wall.

c) Tortoise shell was cut and polished to make arrowheads. A craftsman could make twenty-four arrowheads from one tortoise as well as eat the tortoise afterwards.

7 Stones were catapulted over castle walls to crush people and dead horses to give them disease. What else was thrown?
a) Human heads to terrify defenders.
b) Wild animals to attack defenders.
c) Poisoned wine to kill off defenders.

8 A great lord may have more than one castle. He could move around and live for a few months in each of his castles. How could he stop his castles being robbed while he was away?
a) Leave an armed guard at each castle to keep thieves out.
b) Leave the peasants of the local village to watch the castle – if anything went missing they were punished.
c) He only had one lot of furniture, kitchen fittings, plates and decorations. He took them all with him every time he moved.

9 Some castles had special traps for invaders. What did they do?
a) Opened a hole in the floor and dropped the attacker straight into a dungeon.
b) Opened a gap in the drawbridge and dropped them straight into the moat.
c) Had a collapsible toilet seat that dropped them into the drains.

10 A battering ram could cause a lot of damage to your castle walls. If you couldn't stop the battering then how could you make it less damaging?

a) Throw a box of woodworm over the tip of the ram so they eat it away and it crumbles.

b) Lower a bale of straw over the walls so the ram is battering a straw cushion.

c) Lower ropes over the end of the ram and pull it upwards.

I DON'T KNOW IF IT'S GOING TO WORK BUT I THINK WE'VE INVENTED BREAK-FAST CEREAL!

Answers: How did your pestered parent or troubled teacher score? Here are the answers PLUS some smart comments for the ones they get wrong.

1c) Early castles covered their walls with leather. Great idea, shame it didn't work. The attackers found they could throw the leather over the spikes and it actually *helped* them to get over the top.

2b) Water. Oh, yes, most people *think* they poured boiling oil on attackers but that's *highly* unlikely. Oil was *much* too rare and *very* expensive. The defenders would use water – either hot or cold. This would also put out the fires that attackers built at the base of the walls. Quicklime was also popular stuff. This blinded, choked or burned the skin of attackers when it was poured down on them.

3a) Human hair was plaited into a rope and it had a lot of spring in it. This was one time when long-haired women were more useful to the defenders than bald-headed men. Of course, any dead defenders would have to have a hair cut before they were buried!

4c) Disgusting but true. Of course, you would take your clothes from the garderobe and spend the rest of the day smelling like a toilet. But since people didn't take a lot of baths they might not notice. Your clothes might smell like a toilet but *you* might smell worse!

5b) The towers were made of wood and covered with animal skins. The skins could be soaked in water so the defenders couldn't set fire to your *malvoisin* tower.

6b) The Romans used the word *testudo* – meaning 'tortoise' – for a covering of shields over the backs of attacking soldiers. Soldiers of the Middle Ages had probably never seen a tortoise (and certainly would never have eaten one) but the word was still used to mean a back cover.

7a) The heads were from captured defenders, of course. You didn't go around chopping up your own spare soldiers. You never knew when one of them might come in handy. They also threw hives full of bees into towns (which is fine if you happen to like honey!).

8c) The Duke of Northumberland moved three times a year in the 1500s. He took beds, tables, chairs and kitchen equipment on a procession of 18 carts. (Maybe he didn't like sleeping in a strange bed!)

9a) This is why you should always be careful when a knight says, 'Why not drop in and see me some time?'

10b) This was a clever idea but can't have delayed the attackers for long … unless the attackers were tired, in which case this could be the last straw!

Creepy castles

Ruined castles are spooky places to visit. It could be because they are haunted by the ghosts of the people who died there. The worst times of all were between 1135 and 1154, when King Stephen and the Empress Matilda fought for the throne of England.

The early Norman kings had been very careful not to allow great barons to build too many strong castles, otherwise they would become more powerful than the king. But during the wars between the last Norman king, Stephen, and his rival queen, Matilda, the barons did more or less what they wanted. Castles sprang up like mushrooms in a damp, dingy cupboard. (The next king, Henry II, had 1,100 of these illegal castles knocked down.)

The *Anglo Saxon Chronicle* of the time described the 19 years of Stephen's war as a time for building the most evil castles. These castles were not just homes for the barons – they were places of terror and torture...

> *Every powerful man built his castle and held it against King Stephen. They filled the country with castles. The poor people of the country suffered from the work. When the castles were built they were filled with devils and wicked men. Then by day and by night they took any people they thought had some wealth – men and women – they put them in prison and tortured them with terrible tortures to get their gold and silver. No one was ever tortured as they were. Knotted ropes were put around their heads and twisted till they penetrated to the brains. They put them in prisons where there were adders and snakes and toads and killed them like that. Some they put in a torture chamber, that was a chest that was short, narrow and shallow. They put sharp stones in it and pressed the lid shut till a man had all his limbs broken. Many thousands were killed by starvation.*

So, next time you go on a boring school trip to a ruined castle, entertain your friends and your teachers with some tales of terror and torture. (Just make sure that when they're sick they aren't facing in your direction.)

Death in Devon

Maybe it's something in the ancient stones. Maybe it's just imagination. But some places make the hair on the back of your neck start to bristle. Fear runs down your neck like a cold slug when you step inside the awesome walls. You just know that the place has terrible tales to tell.

Tales like the ghost of Berry Pomeroy Castle in Devon...

Doctor Farquhar stepped down from his carriage and walked over the gravel to the great front door. A rusting iron ring hung next to it. He pulled it and heard a cracked bell clang somewhere deep inside the tower.

The door creaked open and an old man looked at the doctor through damp and faded eyes. 'Thank you for coming at this time of night, Doctor,' he wheezed in a voice as thin as the east wind.

'It's my pleasure, Mr Harris,' the doctor replied, and

stepped into the gloomy, candle-lit hallway and took off his hat.

The men's footsteps echoed off the dark oak panels of the walls as they passed through the hall and climbed the wide stone stairway. 'You must have an army of servants to keep this place clean,' Doctor Farquhar said.

The old man gripped the cold stone rail and climbed slowly. 'Girls from the village come up every morning,' he croaked. 'But none of them will stay the night.'

'It is a little damp at this time of year,' the doctor nodded.

'It's not the damp that puts them off,' the castle steward whispered, but said no more.

'And the damp can't be doing your wife any good,' the young doctor said. 'No wonder his lordship likes to spend the winter in France.'

The steward simply bowed his white-haired head and pushed open a door to a dim bedroom that was lit only by a feeble fire in a huge hearth. 'I'll leave you to it, Doctor,' the old man said and closed the door behind him.

Half an hour later the doctor came out of the room and walked slowly down the stairs. 'She's not too bad,' he said as he met Harris in the hall. 'She's over the worst and should be on her feet in a few days. It's as well you called me. I gave her a sleeping draught and I'll call back first thing in the morning.'

The young man walked across to his carriage as moon-shadows chased one another across the roadway. He shrugged himself deeply into his thick overcoat as an icy wind made him shiver suddenly.

The castle looked more cheerful in the morning light. The door was answered by an apple-cheeked girl who said, 'Will you wait in the library, sir? Mr Harris is just giving the gardeners some instructions.'

Doctor Farquhar stepped into a room flooded with the

morning light. Ancient leather books filled shelves on every wall. In one corner a stairway led upwards to another room above. He settled into an armchair and picked up a book from the table beside him.

He was so intent on reading that he didn't hear the door open or close. But the movement caught the corner of his eye. He looked up and saw a woman glide across the floor. He was no expert on dresses but he guessed her costume was in fashion over 300 years before. The doctor was extremely polite and rose to his feet as he said, 'Good morning.'

The woman did not seem to hear him. She moved almost silently across the floor, the only sound was the swishing of the silk dress. When she reached the stairs she began to climb them but still gave no sign of having seen the doctor. As she reached the top step she turned; a beam of light from the tall narrow window caught her beautiful face. Doctor Farquhar gasped as he saw that it was twisted with misery and pain.

'Can I...' he began to speak but she had disappeared round the corner at the top of the stairs. He sat down weakly and licked his dry lips.

The door clicked open and the old steward walked in. 'Sorry to keep you, Doctor ... are you all right, Doctor? You look a little pale.'

'A party,' the young man mumbled. 'Are you having a fancy dress party or something?'

'No-o,' Harris said. 'It is some years since his lordship used Berry Pomeroy for a party.'

'Then who was the woman in the old dress?' he asked weakly. 'She looked so miserable.'

It was the old man's turn to become ashen-faced. He sank into an armchair opposite the doctor. 'You have seen the phantom, Doctor. Oh, my poor Isabel!'

'Isabel? Your wife? No, it wasn't your wife I saw!'

The old man's eyes were washed with tears. 'I mean my wife will die. You have seen the phantom lady. An evil, evil woman who walks this castle. She lived such a sinful life she was doomed to wander this castle for all time! She died 400 years ago.'

'But what has this to do with your wife?' the doctor asked softly.

Old Harris brushed away the tears and looked at the young man. 'She is only seen when there is a death in the castle,' he explained.

Doctor Farquhar jumped to his feet and hurried to the door. 'Your wife's getting better!' he cried. He tore open the door and hurried through the hall. 'She's in no danger!' he called as he leapt up the stairs two or three at a time.

When he reached the bedroom door he clattered through clumsily and rushed to the bedside. The woman lay peacefully in the cold sheets. The doctor touched her icy hand. Nothing moved in the room. But forever after Doctor Farquhar swore he heard the sound of a rustling silk dress.

Ghostly guidebook

It seems every castle has its own story to tell. Here are a few of the creepiest castles in Britain...

Berkeley Castle, Gloucestershire

KING EDWARD II OF ENGLAND WAS CAPTURED AND LOCKED IN THIS ROOM. HIS CAPTORS DIDN'T WANT TO BE ACCUSED OF MURDER SO THEY TRIED TO MAKE SURE THAT HE CAUGHT A DISEASE. THEY SENT THE CASTLE SEWAGE THROUGH HIS ROOM. IT DIDN'T WORK... SO ONE NIGHT HIS JAILERS PUSHED A RED HOT POKER THROUGH HIS BODY FROM UNDERNEATH SO THE WOUND WOULDN'T SHOW. HIS SCREAMS CAN STILL BE HEARD SOME NIGHTS...

YEOWW!

Pontefract Castle, West Yorkshire

RICHARD II DIED IN THIS ROOM, THOUGH NO-ONE BUT HIS MURDERERS KNOW HOW. SOME SAY HE WAS AT DINNER HERE WHEN A KNIGHT AND SEVEN MEN RUSHED IN WITH AXES. RICHARD FOUGHT THEM OFF SO WELL THAT FOUR WERE KILLED AND THE OTHERS RAN OFF. THEY THEN FASTENED UP THE ROOM AND LET THE KING STARVE TO DEATH. IF YOU SEE A GHOST THEN GIVE THE POOR THING A PIECE OF CHOCOLATE!

RUMBLE RUMBLE

The Tower of London

HERE AT THE FOOT OF THIS STAIRCASE TWO SKELETONS WERE FOUND. THEY ARE BELIEVED TO BE THE TWO PRINCES, EDWARD AGED 12 AND RICHARD AGED 9, WHO DIED SOME TIME AFTER THEIR UNCLE BECAME KING RICHARD III IN 1483. THE YOUNGSTERS WERE SMOTHERED IN THEIR BEDS AND BURIED DOWN HERE SO THEY COULD NEVER GROW UP TO TAKE THE THRONE. SOME NIGHTS YOU CAN STILL HEAR THEIR LAUGHTER AS THEY PLAY THEIR CHILDHOOD GAMES!

Hylton Castle, Tyne & Wear

ROGER SKELTON WAS A STABLE LAD AT THIS CASTLE IN 1609. HE WAS KILLED BY LORD ROBERT HILTON WHEN HIS LORDSHIP WAS FURIOUS BECAUSE ROGER WAS TOO SLOW BRINGING HIS HORSE. HE SPEARED THE BOY WITH A HAY FORK AND THREW HIS BODY INTO THE CASTLE POND. LORD HILTON WAS FOUND NOT GUILTY OF MURDER – AFTER ALL, THE JUDGE WAS ANOTHER KNIGHT – SO THE SPIRIT OF POOR ROGER WANDERS THE CASTLE CRYING, "I'M COLD, SO COLD!"

BRRRR!

Arundel Castle, Sussex

THIS IS THE OLD HOME OF THE DUKES OF NORFOLK SINCE 1580, THOUGH PARTS OF THE CASTLE ARE MUCH OLDER. A PHANTOM WHITE BIRD IS SAID TO APPEAR JUST BEFORE THE DUKE DIES. THE SPIRIT OF A GIRL DRESSED IN WHITE IS SEEN TO THROW ITSELF OFF HIORNE'S TOWER. THE GIRL IS SAID TO HAVE DONE THIS HUNDREDS OF YEARS AGO WHEN HER LOVER DESERTED HER AND THAT ISN'T THUNDER YOU CAN HEAR... IT'S THE PHANTOM SOUND OF THE CANNON THAT BATTERED THE WALLS IN 1648

BOOOM!

Cortachy Castle, Scotland

A CHIEFTAIN APPEARED AT THIS CASTLE ONE EVENING DURING THE MIDDLE AGES. HE WAS CARRYING A DRUM AND BEARING AN UNPLEASANT MESSAGE. THE OGILVY FAMILY WHO OWNED THE CASTLE HAD HIM STUFFED INTO HIS OWN DRUM AND THROWN OVER THE BATTLEMENTS. AS HE FELL TO HIS DEATH HE CURSED THEM AND PROMISED TO HAUNT THEM FOREVER MORE. GHOSTLY DRUMMING IS HEARD EVERY TIME AN OGILVY DIES...

153

Glamis Castle, Scotland

THIS IS THE MOST HAUNTED CASTLE IN THE WORLD! THE DEVIL VISITED HERE ONE DAY AND WON THE EARL OF STRATHMORE'S SOUL IN A GAME OF DICE. YOU CAN STILL HEAR THEM RATTLE IN THE DEAD OF NIGHT. LORD JAMES DOUGLAS'S GHOST WANDERS THE ROOMS AFTER HIS WIFE POISONED HIM. SHE WAS LATER BURNED AT THE STAKE FOR TRYING TO POISON KING JAMES V OF SCOTLAND AND HER SPIRIT WANDERS ROUND, WRAPPED IN FLAMES. WE HAVE A TONGUELESS WOMAN AND EVEN A BLOOD-SUCKING VAMPIRE! LORD MACBETH MURDERED KING DUNCAN HERE AND THE BLOOD-STAINS ARE STILL ON THE FLOOR!

Did you know…?

A group of Muslims who fought against the Crusaders were known as the Assassins. They were led by the Old Man of the Mountains and their job was not to kill Christians in battle: it was to get close to enemy leaders and murder them. They were fearless and ready to die for their cause.

The Assassins murdered Crusader Commander Conrad. Then the Old Man of the Mountains died and a new leader took his place. The new Old Man (you know what I mean) wanted to say 'Sorry' for killing Conrad so he invited the Crusader leader, Henry of Champagne, to visit him. He said he would show Henry how brave the Assassins were. Two young men stood on the walls of the Assassin castle, the Old Man raised a hand … and the young men threw themselves to their deaths at the foot of the c astle walls.

The Old Man asked if Henry wanted to see more. Henry didn't.

Henry went home a bit shaken. But not long afterwards he was standing at a window in his castle. He stepped backwards, slipped ... and fell to his death at the foot of the castle walls.

Weird!

Savage sieges

A castle is a home, an army camp, a local government office, a lookout place, a jail and a food store. With so much happening in one place it has one big weakness: capture a castle and you control all of its lands.

Castle owners knew this, of course, so they made their castles too strong to capture. They built higher, thicker walls. Attackers built bigger climbing towers to get over the walls or bigger catapults to batter them down.

But, if the attackers had plenty of time, there was another way of defeating the people in the castle. Surround it. Let no one in or out – let no *food* in – and wait till the people inside starve. That's a siege.

The most famous siege in history was probably the Siege of Troy. The Greeks ended the ten-year siege by using the wooden horse trick. The trouble is, everyone has heard that story. No one is likely to fall for it again, though in the 1130s King Stephen did pretend to leave the siege at Harptree Castle. When the defenders chased after him Stephen turned round and captured their empty castle!

Could you find a way to take a castle? Or could you defend it? Try this quick quiz to see if you're a Siege Survivor or a Siege Sufferer...

1 You are in Aiguillon, France, and the year is 1346. You are the English commander inside the castle and the French are surrounding you. The French have built a

dozen catapult machines to throw boulders inside your walls. Are you just going to sit there and let it happen? Come up with a plan to stop the boulder bombardment. Clue: You have a good supply of wood inside the castle and good workmen.

2 You are in Wallingford, England, in 1152. You are defending the castle and you know that an enemy army is on the way. You have lots of crops in the fields around the castle. The castle will hold out against an attack but you are afraid that a long siege would starve your people. What two things must you do before the enemy arrives in two days' time? Clue: You have more soldiers than the enemy who will be arriving.

3 You are in St Andrews, Scotland, in 1546. You are defending well but are afraid that the enemy will find a way to get into the castle. You suspect they will try to dig

beneath your walls and pop up inside. But which direction will the tunnel come from? And how will you stop the attack? Clue: They can't dig under your walls without making the ground tremble a little.

4 You are in the castle on the Greek island of Rhodes in 1440. You are being attacked by Egyptians using tall wooden towers on wheels. They begin by smoothing the ground so the towers have a level road. After all, if the tower tilts too far it will topple over. You try to dig ditches to stop the towers coming forward but the strong attackers drive you back into the castle and fill the ditches in. The smooth road is almost complete. Tomorrow the towers full of men will roll forward and they will climb over your walls. Wet animal hides will stop you setting fire to its roof. What can you do? Clue: How would you catch an elephant?

5 You are in Ballon Castle, France, in 1098. You are surrounded by Count Fulk's army and you are getting hungry. The attackers are good soldiers and guard their camp well at night. But you suspect they get careless at dinner time. If you attack them as they sit down to dinner then you have a good chance of winning. The trouble is, you don't know what time they have their dinner. How can you find out? Clue: James Bond would know.

6 You are in Hosn Al Akrad in the Holy Land in 1099. You are Turks surrounded by Crusaders who will massacre you if they get inside. All you have are your sheep inside the castle with you. They are not savage fighting sheep, but they may be useful in helping you to escape. How? Clue: The Crusaders have very little food with them.

159

Answers: **1** Build your own catapults from wood and fire back at the French. The more boulders they throw at you the more boulders you have to throw back. They can't see where your catapults are because they are hidden behind your walls. But you can see *their* catapults from your viewing posts on top of your towers. Aim at their catapults! The result? In 1346 all 12 French catapults were destroyed by the defenders and the siege failed.

2 Harvest all the crops from the fields and take them into the castle, not the barns on the farms. Not only will it give you plenty of food, the attackers will arrive to find nothing for them to eat. Then … *don't* sit in the castle and wait to be surrounded. Hide *outside* the castle. The enemy will arrive, surround the castle and then you surround them! The enemy will be attacked on both sides – from inside the castle and from outside. They'll be squeezed and battered between the two. And that's what happened in 1152.

3 Place jars of water on the ground and space them out. If the water in one trembles then you know where the mine is. You could build a wooden wall around the spot quickly so the attackers pop up and find they are in a trap. At Saint Andrews the defenders dug their own mine and headed down to meet the attackers' mine. A fire underground smoked out the attackers and spoiled their plan.

4 Wait until the night before the attack. Dig a deep hole where the tower road meets your walls. Then cover the hole with thin wood and cover the wood with soil. The towers will roll forward and the attackers will see no ditches or holes in their way. When it finally reaches your walls the weight of the tower and men will send it crashing through the surface into your trap. The tower will tilt and the attackers be thrown to the ground or trapped in the three-storey house on wheels. Then you can set fire to it. The defenders' plan worked.

5 The defenders dressed as beggars and went into the attackers' camp as spies. They discovered that everyone ate at the same time and found out what time that was. They reported back to the defenders who surrounded the attackers as they munched their meal. The idea was a complete success.

6 Release some of the sheep as it gets dark. The starving attackers chase after the sheep, who run for their pastures in the hills. The attackers run after them. While they are gone you sneak away in the darkness and leave the fortress defended by the rest of the sheep. Next day when the Crusaders attacked, they wondered why the Turks didn't fight back! This was one battle where the Crusaders won a glorious victory but not a single human was killed or captured on either side.

Top tips for takeovers

So now you know how to defend your house if it is ever besieged. But what about if you wanted to actually *capture* some fortified place? Here are a few tricks that worked...

1 Wait. Go close to the walls of the enemy castle and let them shoot at you. Make sure that you have good shields to catch the arrows. After a time they will have used up all of their arrows! That's when you pour arrows and javelins of your own at the defenders and drive them off the walls. Richard I of England captured Messina, Sicily, in just five hours. But it's a dangerous trick. The same King Richard was riding close to another fort, letting them waste their arrows, when a poisoned crossbow bolt hit him in the neck and killed him.

2 Love. Tell one of the castle's beautiful young women that you love her and want to visit her. Suggest that she lowers down a ladder for you to climb up. When you go up, leave the ladder down for the rest of your army to follow. Arnold de Lisle did this at Ludlow Castle in 1166. But it's another dangerous trick. The castle was captured but Arnold didn't live to enjoy it. When the young woman found she'd been tricked she killed Arnold with his own sword.

ACTUALLY WE ALL THINK YOU'RE SMASHING...

3 Swim. Castles need water and if you can follow the water into the castle you can find a surprising way in. Chaumonten-Vexin in France was a strong fortress with an endless supply of fresh water because a river ran through the centre. Henry II sent his archers swimming into the city at night. The archers set fire to buildings while Henry attacked the walls. The defenders rushed to put the fires out and rescue their possessions. Henry found it easy to get over the undefended walls.

4 Cheat. Ladies were not considered to be part of the attacking force. They could enter the castle for a chat to the wife of the lord and wander back out quite freely. It wasn't unusual for the attacking lord to then politely call to collect his wife at dinner time. The Earl of Chester did this at the siege of Lincoln in 1141. He took three guards with him ... but as soon as they got into the gateway they attacked the guards, threw open the gates and let the rest of their army in.

5 Terror. If you can capture the relatives of the defenders then you can threaten to kill them if the defenders don't surrender. Henry V did this in 1420 at Montereau. He captured the husbands of some of the women in the castle, then built a gallows outside the castle and marched the men on to it. The women waved goodbye to their husbands and the men hanged. It was a waste because the castle surrendered eight days later anyway, and Henry was kind to the survivors!

6 Disguise. Pretend you are peasants bringing supplies into the castle. When you get through the gates, use the delivery wagons to block the entrance open. Your men then rush through the open gates. The Scots captured Edinburgh Castle from the English in this way in 1341. They upset a coal wagon to block the gates open. The door-keeper was killed 'so peacefully he never spoke a word'. The rest of the English were killed.

7 Murder. If the commander of the fortress dies then there's a chance that the soldiers will surrender. If you can arrange to have him murdered then you will have a better chance of winning. This happened in France in the 1100s. An attacker sent a defending commander a gift: a new helmet and gloves. When the commander put them on he died in agony, for they had been filled with a terrible poison. When you are under siege you should *always* look a gift horse in the mouth. Just ask the Trojans!

8 Bribery. Pay someone to let you into the castle. Many strong fortresses have been captured by a traitor who has let the enemy in through some small doorway at night. Ely Castle was set in the middle of a marsh and could not be captured ... until in 1139 a monk let in King Stephen's army. The monk was rewarded by being made an abbot. It is said he had a miserable life full of trouble because God had seen his selfish trick and punished him.

Suffering sieges

A siege may sound like a peaceful, quiet war of waiting. But in fact they could be quite vicious affairs and not at all quiet.

An army was besieging a castle and called on the defenders to surrender…

165

A horrible but true story!

Did you know…?
The longest British siege was at Harlech Castle in Wales. The fortress was too strong to attack, but after months of starvation most of the defenders were dead. The troops of the English attackers roasted beef in their camp and made sure the delicious smell blew over the starving defenders.

Sickly siege stories

1 Catapults weren't the only weapons used in sieges. A weapon called a 'ballista' was like a huge crossbow. The Romans knew all about ballistas and used them when Rome was besieged by a Gothic chief called Witges. The chief was just climbing a tree for a better look at the Roman defences when he was hit by a bolt from a ballista. It nailed him to the tree. His men couldn't pull the bolt out – and they were too scared of another bolt to try too hard! He hung there for the rest of the siege.

2 The Crusaders were excited by the capture of Jerusalem in 1099. They ran through the streets and into the houses and mosques killing every man, woman and child that they met. The massacre went on all afternoon and all through the night. When Raymond of Aguilers went to visit the temple next morning, he found himself up to his knees in corpses and blood.

3 Froissart's Chronicles describe the Black Prince taking revenge on a friend who had gone over to fight for the enemy. He told his men to spare nobody.

> *You could see the attackers running through the town, slaying men, women and children as the Black Prince ordered them to. It was a sad sight for the townsfolk threw themselves on their knees in front of*

the Prince begging for mercy. But he was so wild for revenge that he listened to no one but all were put to the sword, wherever they could be found, even those who were not guilty. I don't know why the poor were not spared but they suffered too. More than three thousand men, women and children died that day.

BUT ... the town records say that this massacre never took place! The attacking army killed very few people. The writer of the history is saying what he *expected* to happen!

4 The church said that fighting should not take place on Holy Days. No battles were stopped by this rule but sieges often had a day off for a Holy Day. On 10 August 1174 King Louis VII called a truce for St Lawrence's Day ... then he cheated and attacked when the defenders were not expecting it! Not a nice knightly thing to do!

5 In a siege at Exeter the defenders had large supplies of food, but ran out of water. At first they didn't mind. They drank their supplies of wine instead. They even used wine for baking their bread. But when the attackers started sending flaming arrows into the town the people of Exeter had to use the wine to put out the fires. That used up their last supplies and they had to surrender.

6 The most fearsome fires were started by a mystery mixture called Greek Fire. This was a liquid fire that could be blown through tubes. It would burn on water, so water couldn't be used to put it out. Sand would smother it (very handy if you live in a sand–castle), vinegar would put it out (so your local chip shop is safe), and a liquid containing potash would also kill Greek Fire. The most common liquid containing potash is urine. (It would be collected in buckets before an attack, stupid. Forget the idea of a castle fire brigade lining up to piddle on the fire!)

7 A siege at Rochester in 1088 came to an unexpected end. The defenders had plenty of food and water. They could have held out for a year yet they surrendered after a few weeks. They had been driven mad by a plague of vicious flies. The insects crawled over eyes and skin, over food and drink. A historian said, 'No one could eat unless his neighbour drove away the flies. They took turns to eat and use a fly swatter.' The attacker, King William II, threatened to hang the defenders if they gave themselves up but showed mercy in the end ... which is more than the flies did!

8 Of course, the Rochester defenders were lucky to have food. William of Malmesbury described a siege at Antioch in the First Crusade:

> *All the food in the region of the city was destroyed so a great famine came to the defenders. Some people seized the pods of beans before they were ripe and others passed half-cooked thistles through their bleeding jaws and into their stomachs. Some sold treats like mice to anyone who would buy them — they would rather have the money than the food. Some too started eating human flesh from the corpses of the people who starved.*

(Now you'll never complain about school dinners again!)

9 Sieges led to the invention of some incredible weapons but the weirdest was 'The Crow'. This was a long wooden pole with a hook on the end. One end was inside the castle wall and, like a see-saw, the other end could be lowered on to the ground outside. But the outside end had a great hook on

170

the tip. This hook was meant to catch careless attackers and lift them up into the air. Prince Henry of Scotland was caught with a Crow at the siege of Ludlow Castle, but King Stephen dragged him back to safety. (Stephen was modest and didn't crow about the rescue.)

10 King John besieged the castle at Rochester and sent miners down to dig beneath the keep. As usual, the miners propped up the underground cave with wood. Usually they would fill the space with twigs, set fire to it and as the wooden props burned away so the cave and the walls would collapse. But John ordered the bodies of forty fat pigs to be added to the fire. The fat burned so fiercely that the stones cracked. But worst of all must have been the smell. Imagine you are a starving defender, and all you can smell is a feast of roast pork!

The last great siege
When was the last siege? 1649 in the Civil War? 1745 in the Jacobite Rebellion? No, 1940 to 1944 in World War II. The British Isles were the 'castle' and the German Navy and Air Force organized the siege.
The idea was as old as the Trojan War. Cut off the food supplies to Britain and starve the people into surrender. German submarines attacked ships that brought in food supplies. German aircraft battered the people just as catapults had dropped boulders on castles in the Middle Ages. The seas around Britain were the moat.
Britain survived … just. Food was shared out carefully with 'rationing' and the people on the island fortress struggled and went hungry while their armies went out and attacked the enemy forces.
Not too different from a siege of the Middle Ages. And there are many people alive who can still remember it. One thing they may not know is that the 'siege' was more like the Middle Ages than you'd guess. For the defenders

left at the edge of the moat – a group of old soldiers known as the Home Guard – didn't always have modern guns. Many were armed with the best they could find in dusty museums.

The Home Guard, known as Dad's Army, often faced the enemy armed with bows, arrows and pikes!

Epilogue

The last knights

The age of building castles in Europe didn't last long –
the first castle in France was built at Doue-la-Fontaine
around AD 950. Then the power of gunpowder finally
made them worthless within 500 years.

Lords built them huge and high so they would remind
everyone of just how mighty they were. Castles were not
just places to live and fight in – they were stone symbols
that made it possible for one man to rule thousands. They
still litter the landscapes like great grey ghosts – their
ruined outlines still look down and, another 500 years on,
we can still feel the power in the cold stare of their
blind windows.

173

Would you dare to spend a night in a ruined castle? Or would the bare walls still echo to the sound of galloping hooves and clashing steel and splintering lances? Do those strange people we call knights linger on in the tumbled stones? Knights may be long gone, but do they still exist in the minds of fighters today?

Knights – men on horses with lances – *should* have given up around 1400 when gunpowder was invented. Soldiers on horses can always fight against guns – but the fights will be short and they will almost always end with the gun winning.

Yet, amazingly, the soldiers on horses with hand-weapons went on for hundreds and hundreds of years. Sometimes they won glorious victories: Crazy Horse and his mounted Oglala Sioux warriors wiped out General Custer's soldiers, even though the soldiers had powerful rifles.

Sometimes they suffered disastrous defeats. The Light Brigade of the British Army used swords to charge at Russian cannon in the Crimean War in 1854 and were blown away. The French commander said, 'It is magnificent, but it isn't war. It is stupidity.'

Still the military men tried to use the cavalry to attack the enemy. World War I came in 1914. Horses couldn't win against machine-guns, could they? The British Army went back to the idea of the man in a can. They invented *tanks* and were ready to face the Germans in their trenches.

In 1916 the new tanks were ready to go into action when one of the most amazing moments in all of horrible history happened; a moment that marked the end of the thousand-year history of the knight: the commander of the tanks was heading for the battle when he was told, 'Pull your tanks off the road.'

The tanks stood aside ... to let the men on horses come through *first*! The brave lancers charged at the machine guns.

An hour later the tanks rolled forward. They rolled over the machine-gunned bodies of the lancers.

The last knights fell as their ancestors would have wanted them to: facing death.